My Own Strength

"MY DREAMS WERE ALWAYS MY REALITY."

PORSHA UNION

Copyright © 2021 by Porsha Union

All rights reserved.

No portion of this book may be reproduced in any form without written permission from the publisher or author, except as permitted by U.S. copyright law.

Dedication

I dedicate this book to my loving mother, sister, and little brother. May this book inspire you to seek and find love that always lives within.

Disclaimer

This book is not intended as a substitute for the medical advice of physicians. The reader should consult a physician in matters relating to their health, particularly concerning any symptoms requiring diagnosis or medical attention. Please note that this book is based on my personal life experiences, knowledge, perspective, and research. This book is intentionally created to inspire and help the reader only. Some names have been changed or excluded to protect the privacy of those involved.

Introduction

I wrote this book to tell my story about how I created my own life experiences using The Law of Attraction. I intend that this book will help improve your understanding of the power of thought. In this book, you will find my input on the power of meditation and speaking love, people, things, and experiences into your life. I intend that you will gain knowledge from my personal experience of finding **My Own Strength.**

Thank You. Enjoy.

"Our original state of being is knowing our own strength, knowing that power starts with self, and knowing what we came to be, do, and create and to fulfill our destiny as we move through life physically."

-Porsha Union

Chapter one

ME IN THE MAKING

As a little girl, I remember being a huge dreamer. I remember playing with barbie dolls and loved how barbie had a two-level house with a nice car and the perfect lover, Ken. I always wanted that for myself. Yes, since I was seven years old, as far as I can remember, I have dreamt of having a two-level home with an SUV and at least two children. I grew up in Florida. Some would consider it a small city, but I like to rephrase; not too big or too small, it is just right, and you will experience all four seasons.

At first, it was just my mother, stepfather, younger sister, and me. My mother and stepfather used to argue a lot. I hated every bit of it. I still remember hearing them scream at the top of their lungs, then shortly after, I would hear blows from their fists and glass breaking. So many mornings, I would wake up tired due to hearing the chaos that took place the night before. Growing up, I was not exposed to true love or romance, as you can see, but there was a couple I admired, and when I had the opportunity, I would watch them so dearly and loved how my step-uncle showed such affection to my aunt. I can recall how they seemed to have everything figured out.

At the time, they lived in Atlanta and were living my dream. They had a beautiful two-level home in a quiet neighborhood. I remember visiting them a couple of times during hurricane season. It is still so clear how I can remember their house being so clean and spacious. They even had an SUV. It was a Ford Expedition. I remember them taking us on a tour through Atlanta, and the ride was so smooth and spacious. This was the birth of my strong desire to live that lifestyle. At that time, I already had the dream of wanting a two-level home and my perfect dream guy, but it was when I also wanted my car to be an SUV with me sitting high and seeing it all.

From my young perspective, they were the ideal couple. My aunt was also working from home at the time. I always thought how nice it would be to work from home. Moving forward, some years later, I lived in a one-bedroom shotgun house that was later turned into a two-bedroom, one-bath home. My stepsister and brother and three cousins had later moved in with us as well. My older cousin moved in after my aunt passed, and to inform you; this is not the aunt that lived in Atlanta, as that is an aunt by marriage from my stepfather's side. My stepdad had gained custody of his two other children, and my two younger cousins' mother was going through hard times. So that is a total of nine mouths to feed living in a two-bedroom, one-bathroom home.

I used to have nightmares about that house, which is now torn down, by the way. I remember the holes in the ceiling and mildew in the bathroom. I can still remember hearing the woodrats in the ceiling and how they used to come down in the house at night. It was as though the moment we all decided to go to bed and turn off the lights, they would use that as their cue to come down from the ceiling. This explains why I dreamt so big as a little girl due to my living conditions.

As a little girl, I also had a natural ability and a natural love for music. I would sing my favorite songs word for word shortly after hearing them for the first time. One day while driving home from church, my stepdad asked, "Porsha, how is it that you can memorize these songs word for word, but you can't do your schoolwork?" I could not answer at the time, but now, as an adult and now knowing what I know, I understand that I simply was not interested in the everyday basic teachings, but I had and still do have a natural interest in music. I often daydreamed about being a professional artist in singing and dancing. I have come to know that music was my first love. The issue I faced was stage fright. I remember being able to sing so well. I used to sing for my classmates. I still remember the surprised looks on my teachers' faces after discovering that I had a natural gift. I also remember the surprised looks on my mother's and stepfather's faces after discovering that I had a natural gift to sing. It was not until I would mess up and then be laughed at or teased that the stage fright began. Then slowly, my love for becoming a professional singer and dancer went out the window.

I was growing up and had lost my virginity at twelve. Shortly after losing my virginity, I was raped, and shortly after that, I became a wild child. As a young teenager, I had my share of boys. I know a lot of us did while growing up in poor environments as I did. But this is my story. This is my time to share what I have gone through that got me here, where I am today. After being raped, I felt so low. It was as though I was drowning. I never told anyone about the rape at the time, but three people knew because they stood and watched. One did apologize for not doing anything, and you are forgiven—all of you, but especially you. As I said before, I was a wild child. I am unafraid to admit it. I attempted to kill myself by hanging myself from a tree out in our yard. My younger sister came out to cut me down. I remember telling her not to tell my parents.

All I wanted was some attention. I wanted to be heard. This was the beginning of me spiraling down to self-destruction and having bad habits of negative thinking. I have come to know that negative thinking is a choice. You can choose to be happy, but it starts with yourself. Because of the Law of Attraction, you must seek happiness for yourself first when it comes to happiness. What does this mean? This simply means to do the things that you love. Whether that is going to the beach, taking a walk, cooking, reading, shopping, going for a drive, traveling, hanging out with friends, anything you enjoy doing without having to force yourself is simply your call to do it now. Me spiraling down to self-destruction in sadness and anger is one of the natural responses after such trauma. Please know that you can get through this for anyone who is reading this and has gone through or is going through such heartache. You will get through this. For me, the start of this was asking. I will come back to me discovering the power of asking later throughout this book.

Chapter two

NOT TAKING ADVICE

In my childhood, I can recall my mother telling me that I was mouthy and moody. At one point, I stayed grounded for doing things that I would not allow my soon-to-be teenagers to do. I hated being told what to do, which I know a lot of us hate even as adults. So, of course, after being told that I was grounded, I either had something "slick to say," as my mother would put it, or I would shrug my shoulders while rolling my eyes and mumble under my breath. I often would say to my stepfather, "You're not my dad!" as though that was a reason for him not to discipline me when I was in the wrong. I have realized that I came off as moody because I simply could not and cannot take advice from those who do not take their own. In my opinion, while living with family members, parents especially, it is hard to take advice from those that you witness not taking their own advice.

For example, if someone is constantly choosing bad relationships but advises me or someone else not to choose one, how can I take the person seriously? I once heard this said, "It's like a pastor over his church. How could a pastor tell his members not to commit adultery if he is committing adultery?" Yes, people can change for the better. I am living, physical, and spiritual proof, but it is important that you know and are aware of what you do and therefore attract. We are constantly attracting something whether we know it or not. I remember always hearing, "Practice what you teach"—some say preach. Since coming into the queen that I am, I now know and understand this phrase because otherwise, you come off as a hypocrite. But please note: there is a downfall when you do not take good advice that is given no matter who it is that gives it. This again explains why it is important to be aware of the power of your own strength—the power of all-knowingness that lives in all of us. When choosing not to take good advice, it can cause you to have experiences that, I like to say, you did not have to experience.

As a child, being told to stay in the yard or come home when the streetlight comes on is advice I could have chosen to avoid becoming the wild child I was. Instead, because of my freedom of choice in this infinite universe, I chose the opposite. I have come to accept the choices I have made, as it is because of my choices that I am the queen that I am today.

Chapter three

ANGELS ARE BORN AND NEVER DIE

After living in a two-bedroom, one-bath shotgun home for so long, one winter before Christmas, my parents surprised us with news that we were finally moving into a four-bedroom, two-bathroom home. Currently, there were only seven of us instead of nine. My two younger cousins were back with their mom. My older cousin was still living with us but was almost old enough to move out. My stepsister and brother were still living with us because my stepfather now had custody, and of course, there was my younger sister, stepfather, and mother. I can never forget how excited we all were when hearing the news.

Shortly after moving in, my stepfather left, leaving my mother with his two children as well as my younger sister, cousin, and me. I remember being happy he had left because, remember, I was a wild child. I took that as an opportunity to do what I wanted to do. My cousin moved out shortly after because, as stated before, she was of age to move out on her own. My stepfather eventually came back to get his two children after he had settled in his place. So now, it was only my mother, younger sister, and I. Once my mom fell asleep at night, I went through a phase of sneaking boys in the house as well as friends.

After a while, my mom had moved on and started dating. She later became pregnant with my younger brother. While pregnant with him, I can recall the dreams she shared. I remember her saying she dreamt he was born and had three eyes. At the time, I had no clue as to what that meant, but I always felt it meant something deep.

At this point in my childhood, we became homeless. My mom was no longer working, and we were evicted from the four-bedroom, two-bath home. My mom went to a shelter. In the meantime, my sister went with her father, and I chose to live with one of my aunts. I honestly remember being unhappy that my mother had again chosen to be in what I considered an unstable relationship and had allowed herself to get pregnant. I always felt she seemed more happy, nice, and caring when alone. With that said, children are prone to feel their parents' emotions, and this doesn't stop. We then grow into adults being able to feel the true emotions of others.

I notice how children can pick up on true emotions behind a false smile. I was always one of those children.

Moving on, since my mom spent time in a homeless shelter, that opened doors for us to move into a three-bedroom house with two baths under a housing program that helps single mothers and couples that are married. This was right on time because my mom had just had my younger brother, and boy, all the disappointment left! He was so adorable and came out watching *Scooby-Doo*! He would not take his eyes off the television.

The program that helped us required that my mom save money to get back on her feet. So due to days of babysitting my younger brother and working two part-time jobs myself, I became so behind in school that I decided to drop out at the age of sixteen. I must honestly admit that I did not take school seriously. After years of struggle, I was so tired of living under my mother and could not wait to be on my own making my own decisions. I have always said, "If I'm going to struggle, I'd rather struggle because of my own doings, not others"—basically, an "I can do bad by myself" attitude.

I then started working a full-time job at a major burger joint. I had to either stop working and continue depending on my mother while being behind in school or drop out of school to work full time so that I could eventually move out to get my own place. The choice, as you know, was to drop out, work full time, and eventually get my own place. I later enrolled to get my G.E.D., but I still never managed to finish. After approximately six months to a year, my mom had a good amount of money saved, and I was tired of the rules the housing program had at the time. We moved out of the three-bedroom, two-bath home and into a three-bedroom, two-bath apartment. We were the first to live in it as it was newly built.

At the time, since working my full-time job, I met someone through a co-worker. He was a manager at another major burger joint and was also in college. I remember falling for him fast because he reminded me of my favorite rapper at the time, Lil Wayne. We talked a lot about any topic. He often told me to focus on school and that school was important. Me, being who I was at the time, did not want to hear it. But, again, my focus was to eventually move out. I remember how we would be on the phone for hours. There were times we fell asleep while still on the phone. But there was a specific night I will never forget. One late night, he called my phone sounding so spooked. I remember thinking something was wrong. He stated he had just had a dream that he was shot and that someone was with him, but he did not know who it was. He told me that he was drenched in a cold sweat. He then placed me on hold to clean himself and do away the wet sheets he found himself sleeping on.

That is a night I will always remember plain as day because a little over a year later, he was killed along with someone he had met, I was told, only two weeks prior. I remember feeling so guilty because I, many months before his passing over, decided to let him go over an old fling that really turned out to not be the one for me. But again, these were my choices. I felt that had I chosen to be with him instead, he would have never met the person he was with or be in the location he was at in the first place. Again, this was my negative habit of thinking. I now know my friend was gifted. The universe showed him what was to come. Remember my mother's dream of my brother having three eyes? Yes. I will talk more about that later in another chapter.

Chapter four

MY LIFE-CHANGING RELATIONSHIP

After my friend's passing over, I felt encouraged to reach out to an ex, Tyrone, who I was dating on and off since the age of fourteen. To inform you, this is not the ex I chose over my loving, passed-over friend. At this time, I finally moved out of my mother's place and had been living on my own for approximately six months to a year. I later became roommates with two best friends of mine at the time. However, after a while, we all were not getting along well and decided to go our separate ways. That is when Tyrone and I decided to move in together.

Because of his cheating habits, we use to argue and fight substantially. By this time, I was full of rage. I grew to feel like I was not enough and often thought about my crossed-over friend. At this time, I still held so much guilt from his passing and again had thoughts of suicide. We did not have food. Tyrone and I would often go shopping in his mother's freezer or would go to her house to cook and eat whatever she had in her refrigerator. There were times when I would go to my mother's house to eat whatever she cooked. One day, I finally said to myself that I was tired of the struggle. I was slowly becoming aware of the struggle pattern. I slowly realized that I had become exactly what I did not want to be growing up. There were times when alone, while Tyrone was working, I would sit and ask, "Who Am I? Why Am I here?"

Growing up, I would not say we were that big on going to church, but we did go for Easter, Christmas, or when my mother and stepfather decided to take my grandmother's advice to go to church to help with their marital issues. I always, since a child, had a belief that something greater existed in this wonderful universe. But I always looked at it as something outside of myself. Shortly after asking those questions, I started to receive these letters from a church up north. I, of course, ignored them and did not think anything about it. I found myself just throwing them away as they came. Then one day, after a long night of fighting and arguing with Tyrone, I received another letter and finally took the time to sit down to read it.

It talked about how God knew my struggles and wanted to release me from the pain. The letter then asked for an offering and gave guidance to do this and that for me to receive my blessings, and so I did. I was communicating back and forth with this church, and it was slowly working for me. It gave me something to believe in again. Please let me advise; again, these were my choices. You do not have to give money offerings to receive blessings. Please know that many churches scam their members into giving money offerings by preaching guilt into their consciousnesses. When you strongly feel you should reach out to bless someone such as a friend, stranger, family member, or church, do so. Don't allow yourself to be taken advantage of because remember, you reap what you sow, and you attract what you are putting out into the universe whether you know it or not. Again, therefore, you must be aware of your thoughts, feelings, and actions.

After finally reading the love letters from this church, Tyrone and I decided to end our twelve-month lease for our one-bedroom apartment due to not having money to pay our rent as we were already behind. At this time in my adult life, I was a housekeeper at a local hotel. There was a genuine co-worker who welcomed Tyrone and me to come to stay with her and her guy at the time. I experienced quite a bit while living with her. It was while living with her that I first experienced motherhood. I found out I was pregnant with my first baby girl, Aaliyah. I will never forget how happy but nervous I was. Even after receiving this remarkable news, Tyrone was still caught in his cheating ways. He would be gone for days at a time. My co-worker would often tell me that I needed to move on. I did not take the advice, of course. I honestly felt that I could change him. She also often talked about how I could not change him and needed to make that decision himself. I did not cherish that advice, but I do now. I have come to know that you can only change yourself for the better. That is what life and reincarnation are about. It is about finding and remembering your own destiny.

Five to six months down the road, one morning while sleeping, I dreamt that I was in a beautiful grassy field. I remember it being windy. I could feel the wind blowing on my face and skin. My crossed-over friend was there. He was holding my baby girl with a concerned look on his face. I looked down at her and noticed she looked sick. She was tiny, and her skin was peeling. I woke up confused and hoping all was well. That same day, I had an appointment. I was excited and had even run into a previous co-worker whom I had not seen in a while. I remember talking to her before being called to the back for my monthly check-up. She congratulated me and was highly surprised that I was pregnant. Finally, I was called to go back for my monthly routine check-up. I remember feeling like the wait in that small room was taking forever. My doctor finally came in to listen to the heartbeat. He constantly moved the device around my belly to find the sound of what was once a strong heartbeat. Then, he asked when was the last time I had felt movement. I responded with "this morning," as that was when I felt movement last, after making constant trips to the bathroom and after the dream of my crossed-over friend. He then said that he was sorry and that I had lost my baby girl. Immediately, I cried and cried and cried some more. He then stated that I was still young and could try again as though that would make me feel any better. This explained my dream of my crossed-over friend. Once again, this was evidence that we are so much more than society makes us out to be. Losing my baby girl only sparked that question in me once again. "Who Am I? Why Am I here?"

Shortly after losing my baby girl, I could not bear the pain of staying at my co-worker's house without her presence moving in my belly. Tyrone was still caught in his cheating ways, and we still argued and fought constantly. Before deciding to leave my co-worker's house, there were times we fought and argued in front of everyone, even during times when she had family members over for cookouts. Finally, he and I decided to pack and leave. I wanted to go back home, but only if Tyrone could as well. My mother and her guy friend at the time were not having it. So instead, Tyrone and I would sleep in my car. It was a 1997 Chevy Monte Carlo. Even while pregnant with my baby girl, there were times we decided to sleep in my car. So yes, we were homeless. Because I did not have a solid address of my own, I had all my mail sent to my mother's house. After all the trauma of cheating, arguing, fighting, being homeless, and losing my baby, I started to receive the love letters again from the church up north. I did not have a money offering to give but was grateful for the letters as they always seemed to be on point in what I was currently going through and right on time when I needed the encouragement.

Chapter five

MY LIFE-CHANGING RELATIONSHIP II

After being homeless, Tyrone and I finally moved into a nice three-bedroom, one-bath trailer. I was still working at the hotel, and Tyrone was working as well. We were so excited about not having to shelter at someone else's home or in my car. At this point, we seemed to be getting along fairly well, but that only lasted for the moment upon realizing there were no more cold nights spent sleeping in my car. Not long after moving in, I realized my co-worker's father, Larry, and his fiancé, Tiffany, lived in the trailer behind us. I honestly was not happy about it. I thought to myself, "Great, another getaway spot for Tyrone," and I was right. He often would disappear to their place or would lie, saying that he was next door but was not.

The cheating continued. I remember how I stopped fighting back, and all it took was for me to confront him about where he had been and who he was with, and he would hit me and punch me down to the floor. I remember screaming so loud that at one point, Larry and Tiffany came to my rescue. At that moment, I was finally grateful they were only next door. I spent a lot of nights crying.

I found myself enjoying writing lyrics again. As a little girl, as you remember, I loved music. I used to write lyrics to a beat that played in my head. It was my way of expressing myself. I wrote a song and dedicated it to my baby girl Aaliyah and Tyrone. I even recorded it with a close friend of his who also had a natural love for music. I remember hoping that song would help him change his ways.

For a little bit, it seemed to start him thinking. He started going to church with our neighbors every other Sunday morning. I remember him coming home feeling good and excited about the church service he attended. He often would tell me that I should attend, but I did not. I was not ready, as I would say to him. I honestly felt it was for him; I thought he needed to change, not knowing it was actually for me. One Wednesday night, I decided to tag along. I had only agreed to go because I honestly felt he liked church a bit too much and probably had his eye on yet another female to cheat with. The church was fairly new and was a small congregation. I went there for one thing but ended up with another. There was a message that also began this story. My story of Who Am I, and Why Am I here.

The pastor was a prophet. I remember the first message he gave to me personally from the non-physical realm. It was that "My wheels were spinning." I was sitting in one spot while my wheels were spinning. I got from that message that I wanted to move but was stuck in one spot. At the time, I did not completely understand but knew it was on point for me, as I knew I wanted out of bad situations but often felt I could not get out. Whether the situation was financial or romantic, I felt stuck.

After my first experience at the church, I decided to continue seeing where it went, as I knew that I was tired of my current living situation. Tyrone stopped going routinely once I decided to. I found myself going every Sunday and Wednesday. I even sacrificed possibly running out of gas just to be there faithfully. I knew that I needed it. I had questions that needed to be answered that I wanted to be answered. I was growing tired of feeling less than and being without the things I needed and wanted. Because Tyrone was no longer interested in finding himself, he again began his cheating ways. We had our share of arguing and, for years, had our share of breaking up and making up. I then found out I was pregnant for the second time. This time I was having a boy, Kylen.

Despite clinging to an unhealthy relationship, I was excited yet again about my new pregnancy. However, even while pregnant, the verbal and physical abuse continued. As I said before, this only happened when I would confront him. I was told that I was stupid and was called the B-word on many occasions that later led to me screaming back at him, which led to him punching me. One night, I ran to the bathroom as he chased me, but I could not lock the door in time. He beat my face until my nose bled. That was the first and only time I have ever experienced a nosebleed. I woke up the next morning with black eyes, and my body felt like I had run a marathon.

No one in my family knew this was taking place. They, of course, knew of the cheating but had no idea the abuse was taking place. My neighbors were still living next door and came to my rescue more than once. There was a time I came home from work. Tiffany asked who the girl was at my place. I did not know what she was talking about and called one of my friends to ask if she came over looking for me earlier that day. I later found out that Tyrone brought other women into my house and even had them in my bed. I always had a feeling that he was doing this but could not prove it.

One Sunday, I awakened to a slight pain in my abdominal area. I still manage to drive myself to church as the pain was minor, and I assumed it would eventually go away. I got to church and found a seat to sit in; the service started, but I later found myself being completely uncomfortable. I could no longer stand the pain I was in. In my opinion, labor pain is the worst pain. Prophet stopped in the middle of his sermon because he noticed how uncomfortable I was, and I started to cry. There was pain throughout my back and legs. I even had the urge to push. I was only six months pregnant. One of the church members rushed me to the hospital while everyone continued with prayer after realizing I was in labor. Once arriving at the hospital, I was immediately taken to the emergency room to see why I was in pain. They told me that my baby boy was breech and that I would have an emergency C-section.

I came out fine, and although stable at the time, my baby had lost a lot of blood. I could not walk, so I was pushed in a wheelchair down to the NICU in the hospital. It was so hard to see my baby boy in what I called "The Bubble." There were IV lines everywhere. Because I had him at only six months, his lungs were not fully developed nor strong enough for him to breathe independently. Because of this, there was also a breathing mask on his face to help him. He was so precious. I called his name, Kylen. He opened his eyes slowly then looked right at me. I put my finger in the bubble for him to grip. I will always remember his tight grip around my finger.

I was slowly starting to feel confident that my baby boy would make it after visitations from the prophet and first lady, as well as other church members. But two days after having him, I received a call in the night from the NICU stating that I needed to hurry down as something was wrong. When I got there, at least five doctors were scrambling to help save my son's life. I remember seeing my baby struggling for air but trying to fight. Blood was gushing from his mouth, and it seemed he was choking. I will never forget the sound of that flat line and the image of my deceased newborn in my head. I was devastated.

Shortly after losing Kylen, Prophet and the first lady came back to the hospital to support me and pray. They informed Tyrone and me that we needed to get married before trying again so that our child would not be born out of wedlock. I listened and thought about it hard, but not hard enough. Tyrone was there during the devastation, but I spent most of my time in the hospital alone. Although I had a church family to turn to for support as well as regular family members, I still felt lonely. After getting home, I spent a lot of time alone as Tyrone was cheating and disappearing again.

The night before Kylen's burial, I received a knock at my door. I answered, but no one was there. Instead, I was greeted with toilet paper wrapped around my trailer and car. The B-word and "congrats dead baby," was written on my car windows. This proved that he did have other women in my home, and they had managed to vandalize my property. I remember crying while sitting on my bed. I had a beautiful cat at the time named Fluffy. He sensed my sadness and came to rest his head in my lap, then placed his paw in my hand. That immediately reminded me of when I placed my finger in Kylen's hand for him to grip. At that moment, I felt and knew that my baby was okay, but the pain of not having my baby physically was still there.

At Kylen's burial, a few of my family members and church members came to show support. I was fine until it was time to go. I cried and cried until I could barely walk. Prophet and the first lady asked if I wanted to ride with them home. That ride was a pleasant one. It was during the loss of my baby boy that I realized these two people cared about me and my wellbeing. Even to this day, I know and believe that they cared. During this ride, they both told me that I had some decisions to make. Since the vandalization and the loss of my baby, they advised that there were no strings attached to Tyrone. They talked about how it was the perfect time for me to let go and move on.

They were made aware of the abuse and cheating I was going through with Tyrone, so I did not tell them. Let me explain. One day, my mother called to tell me she had dreamt that she was being strangled. She explained how it felt so real that she could still feel it after she was awakened from her sleep, choking and coughing. Some days later, we went to church on a Sunday. Prophet came to me in front of the congregation and stated that he had a vision that I was strangled to death. He said the vision was so strong that he could feel it. He also stated that he was not the only one in the building that had that vision. Whether he knew it or not, the other person was my mother. After telling me his vision, he explained how I should not allow Tyrone to continue with the abuse.

Other things were said as well, but what is important is that, again, this is more evidence that we are so much more than human beings on this physical plane. This is more evidence to me that we are all very connected.

Now back to the advice from Kylen's burial service. Other than advising me to leave, they also advised that if I were to choose to stay, we needed to get married because their beliefs were based on living together only If you are married. I decided to stay after Tyrone apologized and said many things I wanted to hear and because I was not yet aware of the importance of self-worth and love. We then got married. Although good advice was given to leave, I must remind you that I, and only I, chose to stay. Again, this was my choice. Because I have the experience of choosing to stay in an abusive relationship filled with lies, cheat, and neglect, I have come to advise, please do yourself a favor and leave. Prophet and first lady were right. I had the perfect opportunity to move on. The universe, Guardian Angels, Archangels, Ancestors, spirit guides, God, whatever you may call them, were on my side as you can see. There was an open door, but again, I chose to stay because of this wonderful free will of choosing. I now know and understand that I chose this due to a lack of self-love.

Please, if you do not get anything else from this book, choose to love yourself first and foremost. It is only then that you can attract someone that loves you just as much. People only reflect who and what they are based on their own doings and beliefs, and people do what they are allowed.

Chapter six

MY LIFE-CHANGING RELATIONSHIP III

Before getting married, I often felt guilty due to the church's belief in only living together when married and anything else is considered "Shacking Up," so I felt a sense of relief after getting married. At first, things seem to be getting a little better. Tyrone was starting to attend church with me. At this time, I no longer worked at the local hotel and had not since before the loss of Kylen but was receiving unemployment. We later both received jobs at a local fair that comes to our city once every year. This was when things started to slowly go south.

While working at the local fair, the mistress that vandalized my property found out that we were working there. I always wondered if he kept in touch, and so that answered my question. This relationship taught me about the truth behind "Everything that is done in the dark will come to the light." I knew instantly when something did not seem right. Because of my feelings and thoughts of wanting to know the truth, the universe would expose the issue every time. So here we are once again, now arguing while on the job. He even went missing a few times while on the job and was later fired. While working for the fair, a co-worker witnessed the heartache and confusion. I remember telling her the issues I had with Tyrone and explained how I had just lost another baby, yet his behavior continued. I even talked about the conversation I had with my prophet and first lady at the time. I remember her stating how she no longer believed in going to church and how I really should just let Tyrone go as he continued to show me who he was. Once again, incredibly good advice I did not take.

After the fair was over, I gathered my earnings and headed home. I often thought about the conversation I had with the co-worker from the fair job. I even thought about how it had been a while since I had heard from the church up north. Since writing the church up north and joining the church I was currently attending at the time, I often found myself praying and talking while venting out loud to myself to keep my sanity. Then, one night my mother called me. She had received a message from a cousin of mine who, after leaving for college, none of us, not even his siblings, had seen or talked to in years. He messaged her to tell me that my aunt, his mother, said to tell me to "keep praying." Now to remind you, this is my aunt who I mentioned had passed over and caused my older cousin, which is his sister, to move in with my family and me back in chapter one of this book.

After receiving that message from the other side, I immediately felt some relief and knew that I was being heard. Sometimes, when going through hard times, we pray and sometimes feel that we are not being heard. Getting that message from a cousin who no one had spoken to in years allowed me to feel the comfort of knowing I was being heard. This led me to the question once again, Who Am I? and Why Am I here?

After this experience, I slowly started to think for myself instead of being a constant follower. I realized that the church did not agree with such an experience as this. I remember being told that "The Bible" says, "let the dead, bury the dead," as though we in the physical should not communicate with loved ones who have crossed over. I remember asking, "but if the entity that came to my cousin as his mom was 'Evil,' why would it tell me to continue to pray?" I have come to realize that we are both physical and non-physical beings—a physical "body" as well as a non-physical "soul." Our bodies can only move if our non-physical selves are in them. Therefore, if you want to call it dead, then we are half dead already. I have come to see during meditation that all things are living; that's life! Shortly after the jobs from the local fair, Tyrone and I once again took that money to move out. We could no longer afford to live in the three-bedroom, one-bath trailer. We were homeless again, but this time, we were able to move in with my mother. So yes, I was back home. My mother was no longer with her now ex, and since Tyrone and I were married, she allowed us to stay with her, my younger sister, and my wonderful little brother, who was now five.

While living with my mother, Tyrone and I did not fight or argue much, although I still felt that he was cheating. I, at the time, was not working, but he was. I was still attending church faithfully. At this time, I started to recognize how the prophet would call the first lady his "brown sugar." I admired every bit of it. I loved that about them. They both were very much in love with each other, and I knew it was not for show. I also knew that they had a lot in common when it came to love, the church, and their beliefs, as well as their children. In my adult life, it was not until this moment, after being married, that I started to notice the affection these two had for one another. I saw true love at play. We were invited to the marital date nights, as I call them. All the married couples in the church would have a night out with a candlelit dinner. This was when I started to notice how my husband was not very romantic at all. The more I noticed how the prophet and the first lady treated each other, the more I wanted that for myself. I even admired how he would open doors for her and pulled out her chair to sit. He treated her like the queen she was. I wanted that. Me wanting the affection displayed from the universe was done to help create and remind me of what I always wanted in a relationship. So, this is important.

I had made an appointment to go for birth control. I had decided to give myself some time to heal before trying again after losing two babies. As I was preparing for bed, my little brother came to me and said, "You have a baby."

I said, "No, I do not."

He said while pointing to my stomach, "uh-huh, in there, in your belly." Remember my mother's dream while pregnant that my brother had three eyes? Yes. Now you see. I, at the time, did not. I did not think anything about it until I woke up the next day and went to my appointment. Before receiving birth control, I had to take a pregnancy test. I gave my urine in a cup then waited for the nurse to come back to provide my birth control, but I will never forget.

She came back and said these exact words "You're not getting birth control today; you're pregnant!"

I was in total shock! I immediately said to her, "Oh my God! My brother just told me I was pregnant last night! He is only five!" I will never forget how the smile on that woman's face changed to a shocked and confused expression. After stating that, I left the room excited to spread the news while still in shock and excited once again, I left the room. During this pregnancy, since still being a member of the church who also experienced the loss of Kylen with me, there were many prayers taking place for my baby and me. A couple of months after finding out I was pregnant for the third time, Tyrone and I finally moved into our own place again with some help from the church. After moving in, he went back to his cheating and deceitful ways. We moved into another trailer park where, once again, there was someone he knew. His old friend Drake was the friend I recorded my first song with and, so far, my only song with; his parents were living there as well. There was also one other person he knew living in the trailer park. Once again, they were his excuses for disappearing.

I have to say, Drake's parents were also a good example in my life regarding how his stepfather treated his mother. I could sense he loved her very much and embraced all of her flaws and all. I even managed to invite them to attend the church I was going to at the time. They were not too big about needing to attend, but they did attend once. I am mentioning this couple because they played a part in my life to help me create a better relationship. They also witnessed the arguments and anger I had toward Tyrone.

I often blamed him for the loss of my two precious babies. I have come to learn that constantly blaming others does not do anyone any good. I have come to know that all things start with me, myself. Please keep in mind; this does not excuse anyone's behavior toward you. They, too, should take some responsibility, just as I should, for allowing the hurt, abuse, and cheating to continue by constantly choosing to stay. Blaming others can block healing. The first step to healing is recognizing that it first starts with self. Recognizing your role in your hurt opens doors for the forgiveness of self as well as of others. I will provide techniques that have worked for me later in this book.

At the beginning of my third pregnancy, I spent a lot of time watching TV and praying. I often watched Tyler Perry's movie *Meet the Browns*. I, in a way, felt that I could relate to the main character's struggle. Like the movie, I often would visualize someone coming along to sweep me off my feet and treat me with love and respect. This stirred up my desire for a better relationship. I later started working for a local pizza restaurant delivering pizzas. I remember going into neighborhoods I never knew existed in my city. I only knew of one and dreamt as a child of living there one day, but entering the new neighborhoods gave me hope and planted new seeds in my longing for a house. I was ready to live a life of luxury. The opportunity for me to see these beautiful communities also reminded me once again of my childhood dream of having a two-level home and an SUV.

Chapter seven

MY MANIFESTED LIFE-CHANGING RELATIONSHIP

On July 24, 2013, my healthy new baby boy was born. I named him Kyle, which was short for Kylen. Oh, how excited I was. He was considered a premature baby but was healthy. I will never forget waking up after the procedure to nurses and family stating how cute my newborn baby was and that he was. On the day of the birth of my healthy newborn baby boy, I will never forget—there was me, Tyrone, my mother and sister, a co-worker from the pizza restaurant, and my little brother. While admiring my new baby boy, my little brother said, "Yep, and you'll have another one a little after he turns a year!"

I remember saying, "No, I am Not! I'm going to wait until he turns ten!"

My mother and sister then asked, "What will it be? A boy or a girl?"

"A boy!" he answered. I remember my co-worker at the time being in awe. We also talked about it with other co-workers once I returned to work. I had my mind made up to not have any more children until later. After the birth of my newborn, Tyrone and I still often argued that he was not as much of a help as I expected. He still often disappeared and would be gone for days at a time. I remember starting to feel a sense of peace while he was gone. I was starting not to care anymore and found myself enjoying my own company. One day he finally came home. We had a huge argument. I ran outside to avoid being hit. He locked the door, locking me outside. Thankfully, I had my phone to call the police. After realizing that I had called the police, he opened the door. We then started to scream at each other, and I said loudly while in a rage, "One day, I will move on, and someone else will be a father to your son!" I said that because I wanted him to feel my hurt and anger. It worked because he then slapped me on the face. Shortly after, the police arrived. I explained to them what had taken place. Tyrone had already left before they arrived. I remember one of the officers showing great concern because I had seen and spoken to him during previous incidents. He stated how I really should choose to move on and asked why I continued to stay. I continued to stay because I felt he would one day change. I really thought that I could help change his mind, but the truth of the matter was, Tyrone had to make that decision himself. Again, all life and everything there is starts with self. It starts with that individual's mind—thoughts.

Eventually, the police found him and arrested him. So, I was finally alone for good with my new baby boy. At this point, I started to enjoy what I call "Me time." I spent time reading the Bible, daydreaming, and watching *Meet the Browns*. I would also listen to country music. I cannot tell you the titles and names of the artists, but all I know is, country music had me feeling in love. To me, country music tells love stories. It's like you're listening to the hallmark channel. I felt so good waking up to my peaceful, quiet home with a cup of coffee and my healthy baby cooing at me. I felt I had no worries.

Tyrone, who was still my husband at the time, was sent to a local prison. He had visitation, so I would visit, hoping he would change. We were once again behind on paying our rent as we were renting to own. I decided to let it go. I was spiritually growing and knew something better was in the works for me. I had a trailer full of furniture that I needed to get rid of. I was still attending the same church, and the first lady announced a family in need of some furniture as they had just moved into their place. Wah-lah, there was my opportunity to give, and I did. I gave away everything. By the time they were done, my trailer was pretty much empty. All I had left were dishes and groceries, which I gave to my sister, who had finally moved out on her own.

I ended up at my mother-in-law's, Sharon. Because it was only her grandson and me, she allowed us to stay but not for long because she lived in an apartment created only for seniors. We then ended up in a shelter. Yes, my new healthy baby and I were now homeless. During this time, I did a lot of thinking. I had once again started to notice how, despite being homeless, I was incredibly happy and at peace in my mind. My Monte Carlo could barely get from A to B. I barely had any money for gas. There was a time the church helped me to fill up. I also was no longer working. I had come to the point of not wanting to ask my mother for any more favors as we were not always getting along at the time. So here I was, at a homeless shelter—the same one my mother lived in while pregnant with my younger brother. There were no televisions in the rooms in this shelter, which gave me even more opportunities to think. I often thought about my questions once again. Who Am I? and Why Am I here?

Because my mother had gone through this before, I was familiar with the housing program this shelter was linked to. I attempted to apply but was told they were full and that it's normally hard to get a reservation. I, of course, needed a job, which was also required. To stay in the shelter, I had to at least look for work. I remember needing clothes, so the director went into her own closet and blessed me with clothes that didn't fit her. I remember her favoring me. She had said I reminded her so much of herself starting out. I am considered petite, so I still have those clothes and can fit in them nicely. I took exceptionally good care of them, so they still look good as new. I was grateful because I used some of those clothes to go job searching as well as to go to interviews. At one point, I even went to an interview for a dream job, but of course, I did not get it because I did not have a high school diploma. I will never forget how disappointed I was, but finally, I was hired at a local store that sells sports equipment. I was grateful that they decided to hire me.

Sharon, my sister, and sometimes my mother would watch my son while I worked. I even had a case with community action to help find a place to stay and pay bills. I did not have car insurance, and my license was suspended. Community action was also there to help me manage my money better and to eventually help get my license and car insurance back in order. I remember conversing with my caseworker, reminding her to include my husband. She had known some of my history with Tyrone and often talked about how I should think things through and let him go to focus more on just me and my son. In a way, I knew she was right as I had again become aware of how at peace I was without him since he had been incarcerated.

I decided if he were to get out and remain the same, it meant it was time I moved on, but if he changed and were ready to be the husband he vowed to be, my answer would be to stay. Shortly after, not even two weeks, I received a phone call out of the blue from the prison stating that they would release him. The shelter had a curfew, and it was well past the hour. After explaining to security about what was taking place, the shelter allowed me to leave to pick Tyrone up but to come straight back, and so I did. I was so excited that night because I was not expecting my husband to be out. I remember that neither of us knew when he was getting out. I just remember enjoying my own company and going with the flow of things, knowing some big decisions were coming to play.

After his release, things seemed to be okay for a day or two. Then, he was back to his normal behavior. He would have attitudes and go missing for most of the day. Because Tyrone went back to his normal behavior, I knew the time had come to let go. I remember sitting in the shelter room alone, praying. I remember saying out loud that If I were to try again with someone new, I would like for my new partner to be more like myself: someone who was not as social, someone who was a homebody just as I was, and someone who genuinely cared and would love not only me but my son as well as if he were his own. I also prayed that, for the most part, he would be faithful and honest as well as spiritual.

The day had come for us to leave the shelter. Tyrone and I had no idea where we would go. The shelter only allowed people to stay for a certain amount of time. A church member's father had his own business doing commercial cleaning and was told that we needed help, so he hired Tyrone. While leaving the shelter, Tyrone received a phone call from the church member, Trae, who stated that his father said to come to his house. We both had no idea what for. On the way, once again, we argued because he was M.I.A. for most of the day, as he had just started to work nights. When we arrived at the neighborhood, I knew it from my time delivering pizzas; I had only been out in this neighborhood once or twice.

Upon arriving, both Trae and his wife were there. They were a couple who were also there for me when I had lost Kylen. Trae's father, James, was the one that answered the door. When he answered, he looked so familiar. I felt I had seen him before. I immediately ignored this feeling and assumed that maybe I had seen him at one of our church events. He invited us in then sat us down to explain how his son had told him our situation, and all he could hear within was, "The baby." I thought to myself, "Wow." He then explained that we could stay until we found a place as he was only following his spirit to allow us to stay because of my baby. It was December 3, and in northwest Florida, it can be chilly around this time of year. I understood what he meant by hearing "The baby" amid us being homeless and the cold weather we were experiencing.

He then had Trae show us around the house and where we would be sleeping. From the looks of it, it appeared that his dad had not been living in the house for long. The house seemed new and was just about empty. It was a two-level home. The room we were led to face the back of the house and water-filled the drainage that sat over the fence in the back yard. I remember saying to Tyrone, "I could get used to this!"

I was working a flexible schedule at the time. So, on some nights, I would allow Tyrone to take my car to work. I knew he was still cheating even while using my car. One night, my tire suddenly went flat while he was using it. I was not able to get to it until the next day. I called one of my uncles to help with possibly changing it or towing it back to where I was staying. During our conversation, he kept mistakenly calling James my husband. He would say your husband's house or out in your husband's neighborhood. I remember explaining twice, saying, "No, my husband's boss."

Due to my tire issue, I also allowed my church's van to pick me up and drop me off. One day while on the way back to Trae's father's home, the church van driver stated, "Porsha, I can see you living out here."

I said, "Really?"

She said, "Yes, this neighborhood looks like a neighborhood you would live in."

"Umm," I thought to myself.

Because my car was down due to the flat tire, James also took me to work and picked me up. Since Tyrone worked nights on top of doing what he did best, he slept a lot during the day. I remember coming home from work and was told by Trae and his wife that Tyrone was forcing my baby to sleep all day as he did. They stated that, at one point, my baby cried until they finally decided to go in the room to get him while Tyrone slept.

One Wednesday night, I decided to go to church. I was so fed up and needed encouragement. My uncle finally managed to temporarily fix my tire, but it still had a slow leak. I stopped at a store not too far from the house for air. I realized I did not have any change or money to even put air in my tire. Tyrone decided to stay behind as he again worked nights and still was not attending church routinely as I did. He did not have a phone, so I called James in hopes of getting Tyrone on the line to explain what was going on. I explained to Tyrone that my tire was completely flat and did not have money to put air in my tire. James stated for me to sit tight as he was on the way.

He finally came to put air in my tire and even provided gas because he noticed that the tank was almost empty. I was grateful. I then headed to church. Once again, I was so tired of my struggle and feeling like I was alone.

After arriving, the service was going so well. Toward the end of service, the prophet came to me and stated, "Some things are being done behind the scenes for you, but to receive those blessings, there are some things and people you need to let go of." I immediately knew what that meant for me. Before leaving the shelter, I had already had that conversation with the universe and knew exactly who I needed to let go of and what. I was just waiting for the "When."

The next night I had to work—as stated before, my schedule was flexible. I had agreed to let Tyrone use my car for work. James again took me to work and picked me up. That night I remember waiting up for Tyrone, but he never came home. As I stated before, he was back to his cheating and disappearing ways. The next morning, I asked James if I could use his phone to call my husband as I had allowed him to take my phone to work in case of an emergency since he had my car. I called to see where he was but did not receive an answer. Tyrone finally came back later that morning.

At first, there were no romantic feelings toward James —until that morning. I remember having short conversations on my way to work but not much to say from work. Shortly after meeting him, I did take note that he was spiritual and looked half his age. While conversing with Tyrone about him, I often forgot that he was Trae's father. It was as though they could be brothers instead of father and son.

To some, this was and is awkward. Honestly, at first, it was for me too. I would never date anyone extremely older than me, or so I thought. I had a history of dating older guys, but they were two, four, and maybe six years older. I would never give any man other than the one I was with the time of day, especially after watching the heartache my mother had gone through as well as the heartbreak I had gone through myself.

So, what happened next was completely out of my character, and I would not change it for anything. I have no regrets about how my current husband and I came to be. I would be lying to you if I said I never did because, in the beginning, I did have regrets. Now going back to why I named this chapter "My manifested life-changing relationship." After realizing that I had grown interested in Tyrone's boss, I prayed, tried avoiding, and wondered why I was feeling these feelings suddenly. I kept these feelings to myself, of course.

One Sunday, Tyrone decided to come to church with me. Service was great, but I constantly felt guilt, which is an extremely low vibration or emotion. In the middle of service, the prophet called Tyrone to the alter. He stated to him that if he didn't change his ways, he would lose everything, including his wife. I remember thinking, "Wow. I am getting signs from everywhere." Although the message was toward him, that was evidence for me that I had been heard. Even after that prophecy, nothing changed about him. I found out that he was still communicating with his ex, with whom he had his first son, which was the reason behind our first breakup as teenagers. He was also still in contact with the mistress who he had in our home while I was at work, and only he and God that lives in all of us knows who else.

So eventually, we departed. That chapter had closed. James decided to text me one night, asking if we could talk. I was so nervous because, yes, I was still married and knew the feelings that I had for Him. At this point, James still did not know how I felt. When we began to talk, James explained that he too had feelings for me but, like myself, did not understand why. He explained, as we had talked before, how I looked so familiar to him, and as I stated previously, he looked familiar to me as well. I had realized it wasn't because of a church event as James had never gone to the church I was attending at the time. He grew up with different beliefs, but at this point in his life, like the few others I met before meeting him, he didn't believe in the need to attend church. I understood but did not fully agree at the time, but I again felt the need to go with the flow.

We decided to officially date. Because I was still married, no one, and I mean no one, agreed to our decision. He has adult children, Trae included, who did not agree either, but because he is their father, they had no choice but to let us be. My family did not agree either. I remember getting a phone call from one of my cousins stating how I should not divorce and so on, and so on. But none of them knew what I had gone through with Tyrone, nor did they know how and what led me to my decision. I was leaving regardless.

Now here I was, in a new relationship with a man who was and still is, a provider, an encourager, and my lover. Everything was becoming so clear. He opens doors for me, pulls my chair out to sit, calls me his chocolate-covered candy, and love's my son like he is his own. He brings me flowers just because. I remember coming out of the shower to a new dress lying on the bed. He is a protector sometimes more than I would like him to be, and I was living in the two-level home I dreamt about since I was seven.

Although things were falling into place, I still had moments of feeling guilty. I was still attending church and was now hearing a message of committing adultery and this and that. I remember feeling relieved while at home but stressed and guilty at church. Because of this, I was not attending as much as I use to but keep in touch. My decision to not go to church as often made me feel guilty as well.

My husband's adult children were also accusing me of things that were completely out of my character. It was being said that they told him I would bring other men to our house while he was at work. They did not keep it a secret that they did not like that I was many years younger than he. We even sat down to talk, as they wanted to know what I found about their father to be so interesting. They found it strange and awkward that he and I decided to be together, especially so suddenly. "You should look at him as a father figure," they said. I even remember them stating that I should respect them as they considered themselves my elders. They were only in their thirties; I was in my twenties.

I remember responding, "You are not an elder as you both are still young yourselves; I have cousins that are the same age as you, and they don't consider themselves as elders." I thought it was cute that his daughters felt the need to confront me about their father. My father was never in my life. I have only seen him once or twice in person and spoken to him two or three times by phone. "I understand your concern," I told them. I would do the same If it were my mother or father. So yes, after deciding to continue to live and date James, I received a lot of criticism.

This was when I realized that I cared entirely too much about what others thought about me. I now know caring too much about what others think is something we should avoid. When doing so, we are giving them power over us. No matter what, someone will always have their own thoughts and opinions on how they think life should be. We all have that right. I have learned, because of the Law of Attraction, to mind my own business.

Again, as stated before, everything begins with you and you alone. If anyone has a problem with who you date and how you choose to live, it only revolves around how they think and feels about themselves. It is only a reflection of what they have going in their own energy field. Who made it a rule to only date someone your age, or race, or gender? No one. Love is love. We all have a right to love who we want and be who we want. The universe does not care how and who you love. It just is. It revolves around you. Me. All these events in this chapter took place in a matter of months and led me to my dream guy. My husband.

Chapter eight

MY MANIFESTED LIFE-CHANGING RELATIONSHIP II

After only a few months of dating, I was still married but was going through a divorce. I was so ready for the divorce to be settled. It had been months since seeing or hearing from Tyrone, so the divorce was going smoothly because of it. Although everything was so much better than the previous years of my life, I still often felt guilty about not going to church and being in a new relationship while still married. I still felt the emotions of being criticized by everyone. One day my mother called and stated I received mail from the church up north. I was again surprised because, by this time, I had all my mail coming to my new home. I quickly went to pick it up, and it read,

Dear Child, let not your heart be troubled. I have not forgotten or overlooked your need. I have not left you. I am with you, it is hard to see the harvest when you are planting, yet I say unto you in due season you shall reap, and that season is close. You do not see all I am doing; however, I assure you that the power of my spirit is redemptive beyond anything of the world that you are experiencing at the present time. Ponder these words and learn from them. You will realize happiness, rest, and satisfaction that has not been found in your pursuits. Also, I say continue to come toward me, and I will give you that which you seek.

My precious child, accept my words with trust, and I will lead you to that perfect place of peace and joy you long for. Cease to think of those who have shut you out or mistreated you, for in time, they will have need of you, and you will be in another place where your values have changed. Continue to learn of me and know me, and I will make clear to you the ways that have seemed mysterious, yet the knowledge is waiting for you.

I want you to desire and love my will because therein lies your true happiness and spiritual inner rest. Therefore, I am answering your prayer in the best way possible, for I am the Lord who loves.

This love letter also talked about me needing to believe that "There is nothing too good to be true for me." I immediately felt relieved after reading this love letter. Because of my situation, I felt that my prayers were not being heard. I felt I was being punished. This letter was so detailed about how I was feeling and answered my prayers so profoundly. From this point on, I no longer worried nor cared about how others felt about my new relationship. I later met my lover's mother and siblings as we were invited to his sister's wedding in North Carolina. It was beautiful. We had so much fun, and they all were so down to earth. I honestly did not sense any judgment from them. I felt the most love from his mother and his sister-in-law, Paula, who was very spiritual herself and stated she could sense that I am a good person and good for him. This helped me even more to overcome the criticism I was getting from his children, my church, and my family back at home.

During pillow talk, James told me his mother told him shortly after his second divorce that his wife would walk through his front door. I am sure they both did not think it would be me in this predicament at the time, but it turns out it was. It is like I was the full package, delivered to his doorstep.

At this point, I was no longer working at the local sports store. I instead had the opportunity to go back to school to get my diploma. I again attempted to go back physically for my G.E.D but decided to take online classes for my diploma instead. My divorce had finally been finalized. I was so free and could feel the heaviness lifted from my shoulders.

Shortly after the divorce, my man surprised me with a proposal. While sitting in our living room watching T.V, James turned it off and began to pour his heart out, then out from under a pillow that sat on the couch was a beautiful keepsake diamond and yellow gold ring, which I still love to this very day! While on his bended knee, he asked, "Will you marry me?" This happened shortly after our trip to North Carolina.

We also found out we were pregnant after that trip. Yes, my little brother was right once again. As I stated before, I will go into further detail regarding my brother later in this book. After the divorce and my engagement, I again felt comfortable going back to church. I went back because I felt that was where I needed to learn more about Who Am I? and Why Am I here? As you can see, I held a strong belief in going to church. I felt the church was my spiritual hospital. Today, I know the spiritual hospital is within. It is self-love. It is always with you. It is with you everywhere you go. It is also at your home, beach, in your backyard, in your front yard, in your car, at your workplace, in your workplace's bathroom—it is everywhere. So, you get what I am stating.

At this point, my fiancé and I were regularly going to church every other Sunday. He agreed to give it a try once more. Now on my fourth pregnancy, once again, plenty of prayers had gone up for me and my baby's safety. My fiancé and I were originally going to wait to marry. We wanted to have a ceremony with the church and eventually our family, once everything settled, but because of our beliefs and the church we both were attending at the time, we decided to marry before our new child arrived. September 29, 2014, was the day. It was a beautiful Monday.

Just as my brother stated, we also found out we were having a boy. He was born on December 15, 2014. He was so precious, and we were so excited. Once again, I cried when I heard the sound of my newborn screaming at the top of his lungs. He was healthy and considered a preemie. After getting married and the birth of my son Mikah, the family slowly started to accept my husband and me being together. It did not take long for my family to see the bigger picture, as the women in my family have a history of dating older men. My father is also a lot of years older than my mother.

My sister got a promotion to store manager at a popular local pizza restaurant but needed transportation. That was my opportunity to let go of one last physical thing. My car. I gave my 1997 Chevy Monte Carlo to my sister to assist her with transportation for work. My husband had a car of his own, but we needed something bigger. So, of course, my SUV arrived. Now I had manifested my dream husband, dream two-level home, two children, and my dream SUV.

I want to end this chapter with this. Since I've experienced leaving one relationship for another, please take my advice if you will. Give yourself time to heal before getting into another relationship. I am guided to write this book regarding my experience to help you. Although my experience of being in a bad relationship, which led me to my good relationship, was destined, I have to recommend that you heal first and learn more about yourself before jumping into a new relationship and marriage.

Although everything happened for me, I still went into this new relationship with trust issues and anger. At the beginning of our relationship, my husband and I argued a lot. There were even times when I gave a swing or two. We can sit today and laugh about it, but it was not so funny or laughable then. I was hurt. There were many times I accused my husband of cheating, and please know that I had my reasons. He, too, had problems of his own, but it was okay. No marriage is perfect. None. If we were not to work out, I understand that there are lessons in relationships. This relationship has taught me the importance of self-love. In other words, I understand the love that I have been craving since I was seven has always been with and in me. Self. This was a new beginning to the journey of me finding *My Own Strength.*

Chapter nine

MY DECISION TO LEAVE "CHURCH."

After my second son was born, I no longer felt the urge to go to church as much as I use to. As before, my husband did not feel the need to go because he was in another place spiritually. Because I was fighting what my spirit was telling me, I was not at peace in my mind and was feeling confused.

"Let go." I cannot recall the first lady calling me or me calling the first lady, but I remember the conversation. I remember her saying, for the sake of keeping peace with my husband, it was okay for me to let go of being a member of the church I had attended for approximately two or three years. I had become tired of fighting with myself and arguing with my husband about the church. So, I let it go. It was time. The universe, God, Cosmos, Ancestors, Angels, whatever you want to call the source which lives in all and everything, had other plans. I had other plans. That source spoke to me through one of the very vessels that I had to let go of.

This is why it's so important to know yourself, as you are the love we all seem to seek outside of ourselves. That prophecy of me needing to let go was talking about so much, including things and people I was not aware of when receiving it. To hear the first lady say that it was okay brought me peace. I had grown to love them as though they were my parents and found it hard to let them go along with the rest of the church. I looked at all of them as my family. They helped me get through so much and played an important role in my journey of finding *My Own Strength*.

Please know that I do not encourage anyone who feels it is okay to attend church to stop going if it is helping you. The church has been of so much help to me in my physical and spiritual life journey. As stated before, some churches do not mean well. Some are only in it for money, but others genuinely care about your wellbeing. This chapter is about my personal decision as to why I chose to let "Church" go. Like my husband, I was guided. Suppose you feel guided to let it go. Let it go! The universe has more planned for you. It is the same as while in school, you graduate to the next level, graduate high school, and no longer attend classes unless you choose to. The church has its benefits, but you are the temple. You are that sacred space.

Chapter ten

Discovering The Law of Attraction

The year 2015 was a year of "shift with new beginnings for me." I had become an "at-home mother" of two children. I was in school to get my diploma, and though I still carried a lot of hurt and anger from my previous relationship, I was happier and more at peace than ever before. This was a time for healing. One morning, my husband stated he felt the need to show me something. I remember him searching for a movie while I made coffee. My husband finally found what he was looking for. We both sat down to watch it together. I then thought to myself, "This isn't a movie; it's a boring documentary." I could sense my energy stating, "keep watching," and so I did. As I continued to watch, I found myself glued to the screen.

The movie talked about the "power of thoughts." It explained in deep detail how before doing anything, we think about it first. For example, before the Chevy model was created, someone gave thought to it first. Before reaching for that glass of water, you gave thought to it first. Before calling that friend, you gave thought to it first, or you think about that friend, then suddenly you run into that friend at a store or receive a phone call from that friend. This was the start of my new awareness of who we all are and what we are capable of.

After watching that movie, I was mind-blown. I could not get enough of it. I watched it maybe two more times that same day and every other night alone after putting my sons to bed. One night, I was in our home office on the computer. My husband had so much stuff scattered everywhere through the office. I happen to look at the bookshelf that also had junk as well as books, of course, but my eyes had locked on this one particular book. I said to myself, "Is that what I think it is?" It was a book called *The Law of Attraction.* I took it from the bookshelf and said to myself, "Wow!"

Holding the book in my hands instantly gave me chills. I remember calling my husband while he was out working to tell him that I had found the book and asking him why he never told me about it. He had responded by saying, "Because I did my part in showing you the movie, it's up to you now to do the rest." I remember the feeling and belief I once had that the Bible is the only sacred book that held knowledge and truth. No. This proved me wrong. There is so much truth to be discovered outside of the Bible. The truth is that knowledge lives in all of us; knowledge is everywhere.

Chapter eleven

THE POWER OF MEDITATION

While reading *The Law of Attraction*, the book introduced me to meditation. It was so much more detailed than the movie. This is only my opinion; others may feel differently. I noticed the more I would meditate, the happier and more peaceful I felt.

In this chapter, I want to introduce you to some of my techniques for meditation. So, to begin, as advised from the book, I like to put on comfy, loose clothes. I have a love for candles, so I prefer burning a white candle. Because of my research, I have learned white candles symbolize purity and protection. It is also good to burn white candles around your house while cleaning, or if you prefer to burn them after, please do so.

I have a special place in my home that is specifically for meditation and creation. I prefer to surround myself with the things I love. Once I am comfortable, I close my eyes then inhale, counting to three. I then exhale, counting to three, four, or six in my head. I continue this until I am fully relaxed. I then give thanks to the universe by saying thank you three times. I then inhale again, counting to three, then exhale, counting to three, four, or six. Please know that your count for exhaling can vary.

I then go into detail as to what I am grateful for. What this does is allow me to take my mind off things that are hindering me. Showing gratitude for the things you have opens doors for the things you desire to have, whether that be a new vehicle or relationship or home or maybe even a job or career. I know this is true due to my own experience. I did not manifest my dream guy until I accepted that I chose to stay in an unhealthy relationship, which then allowed me to see and realize what I wanted in a good relationship. I did not manifest my dream two-level home until I accepted the fact that I was homeless. Finally, I did not manifest my dream SUV until I accepted and was grateful for the clunker and was willing to let it all go to manifest the new.

I would do this at night after I put my sons to bed. However, it was not until later that I would do this in the morning as well, before starting my day. Because of my love for the *Law of Attraction* and all the knowledge I have gained from reading it, I grew to love reading books and began to find myself attracting yet another book full of power. That book is called *Wishes Fulfilled* and is written by one of my personal favorites, Wayne Dyer. This book introduced me to the importance of being aware of how you use "I Am," and this author also encouraged me to add certain mantras to my meditations, such as "Ah" in the morning and "Om" in the evening.

I found myself meditating for ten to twenty minutes in the morning. I would inhale, counting to three, then exhale while using the "Ah" mantra until my breath was finished. I would repeat this for the first five or seven minutes. I would then sit quietly while giving thanks in my mind and then visualize my desire. Because I still carried hurt from my past, I would visualize myself being healed, happy, and at peace. I found myself beginning to forgive myself for allowing someone to hurt me for so long. I had begun to realize that we were two hurt people that had attracted each other. Because I was willing to forgive myself, I opened doors to forgive Tyrone, as well as other people such as family, friends, and my experience of being raped.

When it comes to being fully healed, it should always begin with self. Please take note that everything begins with self—due to the Law of Attraction. Things are not just happening. We are attracting them because of the thought, emotions, and actions we give or receive, meaning the things we do and the choices we make.

I would then end my day in meditation using the "Om" mantra. This sound, for me, is so powerful. I would close my eyes and repeat the steps I have done before. I inhale, counting to three, then exhale while using the sound "Om." When using the sound "Om" during exhaling, I could feel the vibration of this sound in my temples and mind's eye, the third eye.

This took meditation to another level for me. I would begin to see a white light and could feel as though I was spinning or rising. My body was so relaxed to the point of feeling numb. It was like I was no longer being pulled by Gaia's gravity. This experience came about after practicing the daily morning "Ah" and evening "Om." Because of my desire to know "Who I am and Why I am here?" and from the power of meditation, I began to gain and attract so much knowledge and experience from the universe.

One morning I was sleeping so well, but as I was between the sleeping and awakened state, I could hear what sounded like my husband's daughters talking downstairs. At the time, I was going through some deep healing and awakening. I was doing some heavy meditating and chose to sleep in my meditation space. The conversation sound muffled, but I could hear them say, "She's up there in that room." As I began to wake up fully, I could still hear them talking. I jumped out of bed and stood next to it, and then I heard them joking and laughing.

I remember thinking to myself, "What are they doing in our house?" I knew my husband was gone at work, and one of them still had a key from living with us for a few months while they got back on their feet. But as soon as I opened the door, it went completely silent. No one was in the house. The doors were locked, and nothing appeared to be out of line. I then looked out the window; no one was there. I immediately called my husband to ask him if he knew his daughters had come by the house. He said no, and if they did, they did not inform him. So, he called one of them, who stated no, but they had talked over the phone that morning.

When he called me back to tell me this, I was in awe. I had tapped into another dimension in the spirit realm to hear conversations. Whether it was about their father or me or not, for some reason, my energy, spirit, or soul took me there. I have learned because of this experience that we are dimensional. The universe is dimensional.

Now having said that, one night while sleeping, I had all control of my dream. This is called "Lucid Dreaming." I was aware that I was in a dream state, but suddenly, I felt I had awakened. I had suddenly begun to pull myself out of my body, thinking I was physically getting out of bed. While pulling, I noticed at first that I was so heavy. But then the weight slowly lifted. In other words, I was no longer feeling the weight of my body anymore—I was completely out of my body. I was floating in the corner of my room to look back at my body, sleeping next to my husband on the opposite side of the bed. I touched my arm, and it felt so physical or what we call real.

I was amazed as I was trained to think that "Ghosts" or "Spirits" are see-through with no physical touch. Meaning, when attempting to touch my arm, I was expecting my hand to go through it. I then looked into the corner I was in to find what appeared to be a portal. I sensed a being waiting and telling me to come. I could not make out what, or who it is, or was, but as soon as I felt afraid, it was as though gravity from my body pulled me back into physical reality. I then awoke, gasping and looking over at my husband, who was still asleep.

I sat up to look at the corner I was in. I have three mirrors on that wall, which are still there even to this day while writing this book. I still wonder if those mirrors helped me see that portal with the being telling me to come. I did some research and found that this is called "Astral projecting." In other words, an out-of-body experience. Since practicing meditation, these are some of the benefits I have experienced, and maybe you will too.

Chapter twelve

THE POWER OF WRITING

Since becoming aware of the Law of Attraction and practicing meditation, I have begun to attract people who also know of these things I have told you. I cannot recall how I came across this woman, but she and another loving woman host a radio show that used to stream on the Internet. They both were so gifted. They used to talk about things that I was experiencing, which is why I would tune in because I could relate to what they were saying.

Because I was still going through the healing process from past hurt, I took it upon myself to call this woman, as she also had a show of her own with a hotline phone number for listeners to call for a reading. Just as my experience before, this woman read me like a book. She could sense from my energy field that I was still hurting from past relationships and advised me to write down my hurt as though I was writing those that have wronged me a letter. There was still a lot of forgiving that I needed to do for the sake of myself. I had already done what I needed to do to forgive myself, but now I needed to forgive those that had wronged me. She also advised that, after writing the letter, to then take it outside to burn it and to visualize the hurt burning away along with the letter. I took that guidance and thought there were only one or two people I needed to write to.

I was wrong. After starting the process with those one or two people, I became aware that more people needed to forgive. After I was done, I also realized more people I needed to ask for forgiveness from as well, so I did. I wrote it all out on paper. While doing this, I was able to forgive myself for treating people such as friends and family and even exes the way I did. I understand that there are always two sides or more to every story, and again, there is no excuse for anyone to treat us poorly and vice versa. We are all connected and go through what we go through for a reason, and it is always bigger than human words could ever explain. For example, there was a friend I once had as a teenager who was a good friend, but because of something I thought she did, I chose to no longer be her friend. I remember her crying because she was innocent and did not understand why I had cut her off and called her out. I know this was because of something that took place earlier in my teenage years before meeting her. I was still carrying that mistrust and took it out on that good friend. But all is forgiven now. That was child's play. I am a grown woman now, doing womanly things.

Please understand, overstand that all things are energy. Although I was not writing letters to hand them over to these individuals physically, the process of forgiveness is still done as this exercise was only about my healing, and if you choose to practice this exercise, know that it is only about you. But, because we are all spirit, it is possible, due to the Law of Attraction, that they may think of you, or you may run into someone or happen to see someone on the news or receive a phone call. I am saying these things specifically because it has happened to me. I have run into someone who I had to forgive at a local store and had not seen since moving away as a child. I have also suddenly seen someone on the news as they had gotten into some trouble. All these things I speak of are very real. It all depends on you and you alone.

This is something I do regularly. Anything that is done that is not to my liking, and I find it hard to choose peace and forgiveness, I write my worries away. It is also powerful to write things down that you would like to take place and things that are not to your liking. What writing has done for me, even as a child, is to help me express myself when I am happy, unhappy, or frustrated. After the forgiveness process, it reminds me of how much I love to write. As stated previously, as a child, I use to write lyrics to songs. I started to feel myself having a love for music again.

I wrote a song called "Forgive Me," inspired by a dream I had that felt so real regarding a man that one of my aunts used to date. In my dream, he commits suicide. I later found out, after having that dream, that someone I used to know attempted suicide but failed. That, too, inspired me to write the song, and it made sense of why I had that dream in the first place. My husband is the only one that heard the song. I performed it for him one night shortly after writing it. As you know, I have had my share of suicidal feelings, so I could relate and took it upon myself to write that song to express understanding of that emotion.

After gaining the knowledge of the Law of Attraction, power of thought, meditating, and writing, one Christmas day, my mom surprised me with a journal stating, "Today is going to be a great day." I do not recall telling her about my rekindled love for writing, but I introduced her to the awareness of the Law of Attraction. In this journal, I would write experiences I was having and things that took place during my day. I also would write down the things that I am grateful for. Please feel free to get yourself a journal and write. Simply write your worries away. Write about things you are grateful for. Write a list of things you want to accomplish or manifest.

Chapter thirteen

CHAKRAS

One day after meditating, I noticed an indigo orb. After a while, I started seeing it every so often during the day. I would be cleaning, conversing with my husband, or playing with my sons. It appeared as a quick flash. I also would often meditate out in my backyard. While in Nature, I noticed a yellowish orb when looking at the trees after meditating. I later became aware that there are what I call portals but are known as Chakras in our bodies. In my research, I have learned there are seven Chakras within the body and five without. So, there is twelve total, but when doing further research, it's been said that there are thirteen.

My focus in this chapter will be the seven Chakras in the body. All Chakras have an aura. Focusing only on the seven that are in the body, when open, they make you feel so healthy and in tune with your body, mind, and soul. These Chakras have abilities that we all can tap into when they are unblocked. I have found that the word "Chakra" originally came from India. It is well known in Buddhism, Africa, and the U.S. Some focus on four, but most focus on seven. I have found only a few that focus on all twelve, but all in all, Chakras are known all over the world. You could look at them as energy in the body. In Africa, they are known as Ashe. Remember, we are energy, and energy is all around us.

The seven Chakras in the body start from the bottom of your spine and in your thigh area. This Chakra is called the "Root" Chakra. Its aura is red. This is the first Chakra. The second Chakra is the "Sacral" Chakra. It is located below the belly button, or navel, area. Its aura is known to be orange. The third Chakra is called the "Solar plexus" Chakra. It is located above the navel area. Its aura is yellow. The fourth Chakra is the "Heart" Chakra, located in the middle of the chest. Its aura is green. The fifth Chakra is the "Throat" Chakra. It is in the throat area of the body. Its aura is blue.

The sixth Chakra is the "Third eye" Chakra, located between the eyebrows or the middle of the forehead. It is also known as the "Sixth sense." Its aura is indigo. This Chakra gives you the ability to see beyond what your physical eyes can see. When fully open, this Chakra allows you to see past lives, what is to come and can also allow you to see those who have crossed over while in both awakening or sleeping states. This is the Chakra that allows for "Mediums" to channel the other side. The seventh is the "Crown" Chakra. It is located at the top of the head of the body. Its aura is known to be violet-purple or white. Due to my experience, I prefer white. As mentioned previously in this book, during meditation, I have seen a white light. These are the seven Chakras or portals that are in the body.

Now for the others, they are located outside the body. Above the body is the eighth Chakra called the "Soul star" Chakra. These auras vary as different cultures and individuals may experience or have experienced them differently. The eighth Chakra's aura is known to be seafoam green. The ninth Chakra is the "Spirit" Chakra, also known as "Soul blueprint." The aura for this Chakra is blue-green. The tenth Chakra is the "Universal" Chakra. The aura is known to be pearl white. The eleventh Chakra is the "Galactic" Chakra. This Chakra is known to help enhance spiritual skills. It is said that its auras are a mixture of pink, orange, gold, and silver. The twelfth Chakra is called "Divine Gateway." It is known to be the connection to the universe, ancestors, cosmos, angels—all that is unseen to the waking human eyes. Its aura is known to be gold. My husband woke up one morning stating he dreamt that my youngest and I were under a golden arch. I later became aware of this Chakra and was highly in awe, believing that this is what the golden arch symbolized.

As stated before, the information I have learned can vary; as I have found in research in Africa, it is known that there are thirteen Chakras. One is below the body called the "Earthstar" Chakra. It is located below the feet. I personally feel more grounded when walking outdoors on Gaia's surface barefoot while visualizing white light shooting from the top of my head down to my root Chakra as well as white light shooting from the Earthstar Chakra into my root. Please note, below Gaia's surface is where the finest crystals and stones are found. I have come to know that Gaia is a living, breathing being herself. So, when you think of the "Earthstar" Chakra, think of it as Gaia's—earth's—the heart. Becoming aware of these Chakras took meditation to another level for me. I found myself feeling more connected to the universe, to God, to all there is.

Now that I have explained what Chakras are, I want to take you back to my younger brother. After discovering these Chakras, I finally understood in more detail how my brother was able to see me have my two sons before I had them. I also understood how my crossed-over friend could see his passing-over event take place before it happened. I also understood how the prophecies I received came to be. In the case of my brother, most tend to have to work hard to unblock the Third eye, "Sixth sense" Chakra, but he was born with it completely open. I now understand why my mother saw him with three eyes in her vision. Even she could see the gifts her child would be born with before giving birth to him. See, we are all capable of tapping into this power. Just allow yourself to slow down and breathe. Have fun. Laugh. Just be.

Please allow me to go into further detail to provide the abilities each Chakra in the body has when open or unblocked.

1. <u>Root Chakra</u>: When unblocked or open. The Root Chakra can give you a sense of belonging. It gives you the ability to stand your ground and to stick up for yourself. When this Chakra is blocked, it can make you feel as though you do not belong. I found myself feeling as if I did not belong after my rape incident. I later found myself not standing my ground when wronged. I allowed others to take advantage of me. To rebalance this Chakra, as stated before, I would walk out in my backyard, barefoot in the grass, while visualizing white light shooting from the unknown ends of the universe, down to my Crown Chakra, down to the Root Chakra, then through mother earth's surface. For me, this is so much easier on a beautiful sunny day as the sun has its benefits as well. I love to inhale the fresh air from Nature with my eyes closed while feeling

the warmth of the sun on my face and skin, then exhale, putting my focus on the Root Chakra and my feet.

2. <u>Sacral Chakra</u>: When unblocked or open, this Chakra can help you feel and be creative. You will find yourself manifesting ideas and acting on those ideas. When this Chakra is blocked, it can have you feeling out of tune with your natural gifts and abilities, like when I allowed myself to be afraid of messing up while singing or dancing or when I no longer had any ideas for writing music. This later caused me to no longer dream of becoming a professional artist in music and dance. This Chakra also plays a big role in pleasure for sex. For some of us, after going through the trauma of rape, we find ourselves being extremely sexual, as I already was before the incident. Still, I later found myself no longer experiencing the pleasure of sex. This does not mean that I was burnt out on sex. This simply means the Sacral Chakra had been closed or blocked. We also tend to blame age for no longer having pleasure for sex, but that is not the case again. All that is needed is some self-healing, focusing on this Chakra, then watch yourself become filled with orange fire for sex. To open this Chakra, I would wear orange or any vibrant color. White helps a lot while meditating. I would inhale counting to three, then exhale counting to three, four, or six while visualizing white light shooting from my Crown down to my Sacral Chakra. I would even visualize the

white light coming from the outer space of Gaia—from above my Crown. While focusing on these Chakras, I would also state affirmations which I will talk about later in this chapter.

3. <u>Solar plexus Chakra</u>: When unblocked or open, this Chakra can have you feeling and being confident. I have come to know that this is where the power is. This is my center. This is the Chakra of wisdom. You know that feeling you have when you just *know* or that feeling of uncertainty? This is where these emotions live. Have you ever watched something so gruesome on television that you could feel it in your stomach? And have you ever listened to music that had you feeling so good and confident about yourself? That is because of this Chakra. When healing myself while opening and unblocking this Chakra, I prefer wearing yellow. I say an affirmation during meditation and throughout my day, stating, "I Am confident. I Am power. I Am strong." As mentioned before, I would inhale counting to three, four, or six. I would visualize white light shooting from the depths of the universe, then to my Crown and down to my Solar plexus Chakra.

4. <u>Heart Chakra</u>: When unblocked or open, this Chakra can have you feeling love for yourself as well as for others. You will take the time to do more for yourself and others and reflect kindness. Please note, when loving yourself,

you then attract others who love you as well. Your life is only a reflection of who you are and what you have in your current energy field based on your beliefs, thoughts, and emotions. When this Chakra is blocked or closed, you will find yourself hating not only others but yourself as well. Disliking someone else is only a reflection of your dislike for yourself. As stated before, everything starts with you.

When in a relationship while this Chakra is blocked, we tend to attract people who do not know nor understand who we are. They can be very disrespectful and tend to only focus on and point out our flaws. This tends to take place from both parties. This is because like attracts like. What is above so below. What goes up, must come down. You reap what you sow. All those involved attracted each other because of who they were as individuals. This is why I stated, based on my experience, that before getting into another relationship after leaving one, take the time out to get to know yourself and to heal so that you can then attract someone more to your liking. The world-universe really does revolve around you. I could not tell you how many times while growing up I was told it did not; turns out it does.

Some of the things I have done to open or unblocked this Chakra are placing my hand over my heart and sitting still in a quiet place. I would say affirmations such as: I Am love. I Am loved. I Am kind. I Am one with the universe,

God. I would do this while my eyes were closed, visualizing white light pouring into my Heart Chakra like a waterfall. I would then inhale, counting to three, then exhale, counting to three, four, or six. I found myself doing more for myself, such as taking soothing baths. I love the beach, so I would sometimes go to the beach after dropping my eldest son off at school when he started pre-k. I had also developed a love for crystals and stones and purchased one for myself, which I will talk about later.

5. <u>Throat Chakra</u>: When this Chakra is open or unblocked, you can speak your truth. For instance, when you have an opinion, you speak it because sometimes, what may only be an opinion to others can be true to you. Remember, the universe revolves around you. Everything you say and do you attract is based on your own belief and understanding, which is the reason behind why this book is called, *My Own Strength*. Lean not to your own understanding can be true to a certain extent. If there is something you understand and believe and it is something that serves you for your highest good, why not lean on, or toward, your own understanding? To me, "Lean not to your own understanding" simply means to always have room to learn something new. To you, this may just be my opinion. To me, this is true. Please feel free to make this true to you too.

When this Chakra is closed or blocked, we tend to keep our opinions or truths to ourselves. We allow others to speak for us, and when feeling the nudge to say something, we choose not to. Please know, there is a time and place for everything. There is a time to speak just as there is a time to keep quiet. All these Chakras intertwine and work together. Therefore, it is important to give all of them your full attention. When not speaking your truth, it also shows a lack of confidence in the Solar plexus Chakra. As I continued to exam myself, I realized the truth of the need to balance these Chakras after becoming aware of them.

6. <u>Third eye or Sixth sense Chakra</u>: When this Chakra is open or unblocked. You can see the unseen or unknown. You can see the past as well as the future while in a dream or wakeful state. The Third eye or Sixth sense is also your spirituality and intuition. As stated previously in this chapter, my younger brother saw me having two sons before I had them. He was able to tell me their genders and would also tell us he could see people on the other side. I believe him, especially after coming into this knowledge and having experiences myself.

When this Chakra is closed or blocked, we cannot see beyond the veil. You also have a feeling of disconnection with your intuitive self. You tend to not have any sense of spirituality and tend to only focus on what is in front of you, what is currently taking place or your current situation, or in other words, only what the waking human eyes can see. When made aware of this Chakra, I had a better understanding of how my brother, friend, and the prophet saw events before they took place. Do you ever go to sleep, dream, then wake up not knowing or remembering what you dreamt about? But then a day comes in the physical realm (some say the third dimension, some say fourth, while others say the fifth or waking state of life), and that dream takes place in the physical reality, and you then remember what took place. You then say to yourself, "I dreamt of this or saw this before." Have you ever experienced this? I have since I was a child.

I have noticed this take place even more often since meeting my husband. I have come to know that my husband and I have been together before in past lives. This explains why we both looked so familiar to each other the moment he opened the door. This also explains why since being with my husband, what we call "Deja vu" happens so often. Things I have done to open or unblock this Chakra are as mentioned before. I close my eyes to inhale while counting to three in my head, then exhale, counting to three, four, or six. Then I visualize a white light pouring into my Third eye Chakra. As stated in the meditation chapter, at night, I say the mantra "Om" and can feel the vibration in my temples and Third eye Chakra. I then end by giving thanks to the universe for allowing me to see the truth or answer any questions I may have. I then say "Thank you" for helping me to be in tune with my intuition so that I make better decisions, which serves me for my highest good.

7. <u>Crown Chakra</u>: When this Chakra is open or unblocked, you are completely connected to the universe. You can feel that connection, and during meditation, like me, you can see it in yourself as well as in others. Remember, these Chakras intertwine with each other, so when you're grounded, you feel creative and pleasurable; you are confident. You find yourself loving and being more kind to yourself and others. And because you love yourself, you then can speak your truth; because you spoke your truth, you then can see all truth and are very intuitive, and because you are intuitive, you are now connected to the universe, which then opens doors to the rest of the Chakras, portals, of the universe. As above so below. Please note, these things are true to me due to my personal experience and research.

One Chakra may be closed while others are open. For instance, you may feel confident about something but do not speak your truth, or you may feel and be completely connected to the universe, but you don't feel grounded. For me, either/or is true as nothing is impossible in the universe. We are never completely shut off from the universe as we are the universe ourselves.

When the Crown is closed or blocked, you tend to feel and be closed-minded. You also feel that you are less fortunate and are materialistic. You also carry a lot of fear, which explains why, during my out-of-body experience, the moment I felt fear, I was quickly drawn back to the body. This Chakra, when blocked, can also make it hard to learn. Some of the things I have done to open or unblock this Chakra is as stated before. I close my eyes to then inhale, counting to three, four, or six. I would then be silent while sitting still in a comfortable place in my home, visualizing white light flowing and pouring into my Crown Chakra, which again is located at the top of the head of the body. I would then inhale, counting to three, and exhale, counting to three, four, or six.

I would repeat this until I am fully relaxed. I would then state affirmations such as: I Am connected. I Am intelligent. I Am unique. I Am God. I Am the universe. When exhaling, I would say the "Om" mantra. I now know that it was this Chakra with this mantra along with the Third eye Chakra opening that allowed me to have the out-of-body experience. As stated, the moment I started to fear after seeing the portal with a presence ushering me to come, I instantly was drawn back into my body and could feel Gaia's gravity pulling my "Astral body" back in. This caused me to awaken out of physical sleep. I know and understand that I am a soul. I am non-physical in a physical body. I now know and understand this is my reason for being here. This answered my question, "Who Am I, and Why Am I here?" I am here to have these experiences and to then share them with you with the intent of helping you on your journey of finding your own strength. Here are some affirmations for each of all seven Chakras in the body.

1. Root Chakra: I Am rooted. I Am grounded. I Am secure. I Am safe. I belong.

2. Sacral Chakra: I Am creative. I Am pleasurable. I Am Happy. I Am enjoyable. I enjoy life.

3. Solar plexus Chakra: I Am wise. I Am wisdom. I Am Confident. I Am power. I Am strong.

4. Heart Chakra: I Am love. I Am loved. I Am Kind. I love myself and others. I Am kind to myself and others.

5. Throat Chakra: I speak the truth. I speak my truth. I speak with clarity. I speak clarity. I speak love. I speak with love.

6. Third eye Chakra: I see the truth. I Am intuitive. I Am spiritual. I Am my inner guidance. I trust my intuition.

7. Crown Chakra: I Am God. I Am the universe. I Am intelligent. I Am unique. I Am one with pure positive source energy. I Am that I Am. These are affirmations I use during meditation when focusing on my Chakras.

Sometimes, I also state all of these affirmations throughout my day.

Chapter fourteen

MEET THE ARCHANGELS

While becoming aware of the Law of Attraction and the Chakras, the archangels, which I like to call my spirit guides, introduced themselves to me one after another. Since becoming aware of these angelic beings, others have made themselves known as well. I will talk about that in a later chapter. As stated in the previous chapter, when I first became aware of the Chakras, I noticed the indigo orb that would often flash throughout my day while cleaning, conversing with my husband, or playing with my children. Because I saw this orb, it caused me to ask what it meant, what it was, and why did I see it?

While becoming aware of the Chakras, as all of this was taking place simultaneously, I remember hearing "Michael" in my head. I would then see the name everywhere, such as going through ads that were mailed and seeing the store, Michaels, ad or watching TV and seeing commercials. Or I would be out and about and hear someone talking to their child, stating their name, Michael. Because I was already aware of Archangel Michael as he is mentioned quite a few times in Christianity, I began to realize the indigo orb I was seeing, other than my Third eye Chakra being open, were also signs that Archangel Michael was making himself known.

<u>Archangel Michael</u> is a symbol of protection. His colors are often known as royal blue or gold. As I stated previously, the color I was seeing, and still do, is indigo. Once aware of Archangel Michael, I began to call on this angelic being during meditation and prayer. I would also give thanks and an affirmation such as, "Thank you, Archangel Michael, for protecting my family and me. I Am protected." I would say this while visualizing this angel standing tall and firm with huge white wings on his back, holding a sword in one hand and a shield in the other. I would also visualize the white light pouring onto my Root Chakra to feel grounded, onto my Third eye Chakra to enhance my intuition, and onto my Throat Chakra to help me to speak my truth.

After Archangel Michael made himself known while caring for my eldest, Kyle, I began to hear the name "Gabriel" in my mind. I began to hear his or her name everywhere out in the physical realm we all live in.

One day, while listening to another streaming radio show, a lady mentioned Archangel Gabriel; her show was about archangels, and that day she focused on Archangel Gabriel. She mentioned Archangel Gabriel being an angel for children. When she said that, I remembered Archangel Gabriel to be the angel that told Mary she was going to give birth to Yahshua—well known as Jesus. It was at that moment, I realized I should call on this archangel when it pertains to my children and their wellbeing. Kyle was starting to have some major behavioral problems at school, and I did not know what to do. I did not feel the urge to introduce him to meditation as he was only three and would have had a hard time comprehending.

I then started to see green and hearing the name "Raphael." It occurred to me that this was Archangel Raphael.

As mentioned before, I was also learning about the Chakras and the Law of Attraction and realized my love for Nature and Gaia-earth had increased. As stated before, I would go to the beach after dropping my eldest off at school. This was also when I was writing my worries away and burning the letters written to those I needed to forgive and vice versa. I also found myself meditating more while out in Nature. I even took note of seeing messages throughout my day from Nature. I grew a love for red cardinals and noticed how, while sitting in my backyard, they would fly comfortably to sit in the trees and on the fence near me. I was so amazed at how they would examine me while I did the same to them.

On April 21, 2016, the day the singer Prince passed over, I was sitting down at a window looking into my backyard with the thought of the world physically losing an Icon. I had MSNBC on my television, and they had just announced the news. I could not believe it; he was one of my mother's all-time favorites. I got up from the chair to check on my napping sons. I then came back downstairs, and as I was walking back to the chair that allows me to look out into my backyard, a hawk was sitting on my fence, looking right at me. As we made eye contact, I was in awe. I could not believe the beauty that sat right outside my window. This bird was so huge. Its claws looked like four curled fingers. I was so surprised that these birds normally remain in high places and keep away from human habitat.

Hawks can see from afar; therefore, they symbolize clear vision, being able to see beyond the veil, as well as increased spiritual abilities. This beautiful bird sat on the fence for at least ten minutes. I have come to know that Archangel Raphael is an angel of healing, is known to provide healing ideas, and can help promote a love for Nature, earth therefore Gaia.

After becoming aware of Archangel Raphael, I then noticed that I was being drawn to pink. I sensed strong feminine energy and found myself wanting to wear my natural afro; I no longer wanted to straighten or perm my hair. I also found myself wearing my favorite fragrance, and I was getting dressed every morning like I was heading to work. To remind you, I was still an at-home mom of two children. At the time, I had my focus on getting my dream job that I was previously turned down for due to not having my diploma as mentioned in chapter seven. I had realized this was all because of <u>Archangel Jophiel</u>. She is an angel of beauty. Please note, again this is from my experience as some of this information regarding these archangels vary. I have found in research that Archangel Jophiel symbolizes wisdom, and her aura is yellow. When channeling her, I was drawn to pink and sensed strong feminine energy.

There is another archangel known as <u>Chamuel</u>, who is known to be very feminine and whose aura is pink, according to further research. Still, I choose to follow my intuition and guidance regarding this angelic being Jophiel. While doing my hair and getting dressed, I would give gratitude to Jophiel for helping me to beautify my appearance. During meditation, I would thank Jophiel for helping me to beautify my being, my soul, my inner appearance.

Shortly after being aware of Jophiel, I then became aware of <u>Uriel</u>. Uriel came to me with a yellow aura that symbolizes wisdom and knowledge. While getting my diploma, I often would call on this archangel to help me understand my work and studies. I often meditated and would state affirmations such as I Am knowledge. I Am Intelligent. I Am wise. I Am wisdom. I Am smart.

Lastly, I was introduced to <u>Archangel Zadkiel</u>. Zadkiel is an angel of freedom and forgiveness. As stated before, these angels made themselves known to me while I was healing myself from past hurt and abuse. When this angel made himself known, as I was shown many times before, I knew that I was on the right path. This was more confirmation that "All is well." Zadkiel also has a blueish-indigo aura. I was in school at the time I was becoming aware of these archangels. I was also getting guidance to go back to work once I received my diploma. This was only the beginning of me becoming aware that we are never truly alone. There are armies behind the scenes of this physical realm we live in. When you feel lonely, please think of this chapter, meditate, and be made known as your guides are here to assist.

Chapter fifteen

How I manifested my dream job

Since the age of eighteen, I have dreamt of working in the corporate world, but when attempting to get the job, I was declined due to not having my diploma. Because I had become aware of all this power that lives within all of us and all things, I'd begun to focus on seeing myself with my dream job mentioned in chapter seven. As previously mentioned, I felt guidance to focus on going back to work. I was an at-home mom of two sons and a wife to a loving, caring husband. I would start my day early before my sons would wake up with meditation, stating, "Ah." I would do this, as mentioned before, by inhaling, counting to three, then exhaling with "Ah" until my breath was complete. I would do this for at least five to seven minutes or until I felt completely confident and relaxed.

I would then visualize working at my dream job. I would go into detail in my mind by seeing myself kissing my husband goodbye, then getting into my vehicle and driving myself to work after I dropped my son off at school. I would visualize myself parking then walking through the doors. I would then visualize myself sitting at a desk in front of a computer, typing. After visualizing, I would inhale, counting to three, then exhale with the mantra "Ah" until my breath was complete. I would do this for five minutes and end with gratitude. I would say, "Thank you, thank you, thank you for providing me with my new dream job. Thank you, for this is already done. Everything is always working out for me. All is well. Namaste'."

After meditating, I would then get dressed like I was preparing for work. While getting dressed, I would thank Jophiel for beauty and for allowing and helping me to see the beauty in all things. I would then take my son to school. While driving my son to school, I would acknowledge my smooth ride and would give thanks to the universe for blessing me with my beautiful SUV. I would then go to the store if I needed to. While at the store, I would give thanks to the employees for their service. If I did not need to go shopping, if feeling guided, I would go to the beach. Before going to the beach, I would grab a coffee and drink it while on my way there.

At the beach, I would take my shoes off and bury my feet in the beautiful white Florida sand. I would give thanks to the universe. I also carried a stone and would pull it out to charge it with the sun. I would acknowledge its beauty. I would thank the universe for grounding me and helping me to feel that I belonged. While looking out into the ocean and admiring my surroundings, I would say to Gaia, "Look at how beautiful you are." Once I was done spending time out on the beach, I would then go about my day.

I would end my day, after putting my sons to bed, with a meditation using the "Om" mantra. Beginning by lighting a white candle, I gave thanks to the universe for allowing me and helping me to be my best authentic self. I also gave thanks for the wonderful day I had. After lighting my white candle and giving gratitude, I would then sit in a comfortable location in my home to inhale, counting to three slowly, and exhale while using the "Om" mantra. I would do this until I was fully relaxed. I would then visualize myself getting up from my desk, walking out of doors, getting into my car, and driving home from work. I would then again give thanks to the universe for the wonderful day I had an end with inhaling again, counting to three slowly, then exhaling, using the "Om" mantra. I then would say, "Thank you, thank you, thank you." I say "Thank you" three times because it helps me feel the enhancement of giving gratitude to the universe.

I did this, as well as giving thanks to the archangels every day or every other day until I started to feel bored and tired of being home, which then guided me to take action. I put in my application and saw that they had walk-in interviews daily because they needed employees for their new client. So I decided to go the very next day. Before going into the building, I gave thanks to the universe and quickly visualized white light pouring onto my Throat, Root, Sacral, and Solar plexus Chakras. I also carried my stone for confidence enhancement and protection.

I finally made my way into the building for an interview and a typing test. I was so confident during the interview, but when it was time for the typing test, I started to feel nervous. However, once I sat down to see what I was doing, I was fine. This was a big step for me into what I call the unknown. I had never worked in the corporate field before. As you now know, I had my share of fast food and hospitality jobs, and sometimes I come off as anti-social, especially at that time because I had spent most of my time with my two sons. The only adult time I had was with my husband.

After my interview, I went home feeling fantastic. I was so proud of myself for finally taking action to do something I had wanted and was well above my comfort zone. The very next day, I received a call from the company congratulating me and stating I was hired. I was so excited and quickly thanked the person on the other end. I immediately thought to myself, "Wow, this works!" After hanging up, I could not tell you how much I thanked the universe and all my guides for their help. This was the next chapter of my life. My first day was to be October 2.

After getting my dream job, my next step was to understand what the trainer was teaching and to master it. During training, I would write notes, as this was required, then take them home to study. Like before, when getting my diploma, I would meditate and state affirmations. I also would state affirmations at work in my head, such as I Am wise. I Am wisdom. I Am intelligent. I understand what the teacher is teaching. I Am confident. I Am safe. I Am protected. I belong.

I graduated training and was on my way to what was called "the floor." It is where all the magic happens. It is where the phone calls for the client are taken. I was finally doing what I had visualized. For two years, I made it my focus to work at this job. I finally had the urge, emotions that were my intuition and Crown, to act, and when I did, it happened smoothly and rapidly. Please remember, this is how practicing and following my guides have manifested for me. This is my experience. We all have our own way of life, of doing things, and therefore manifesting. So please, if you will, do as you feel with this knowledge and watch doors open for you.

While working my dream job, I met others who had this knowledge as well. I was experiencing the truth of attracting people who also knew of these teachings that I have come to tell you of now. During our breaks between calls or when it was slow, I found myself surrounded by others who felt and thought as I did. Finally, others outside of my husband and me knew of this magical universe we live in. I started to notice this happening regularly as I later found out my eldest son's principal had this knowledge. One day she called for a meeting. I happened to look on her desk to see the Law of Attraction quote in a frame. That alone made me excited. I found myself being happy over what we consider the "small things" in life. You will too. So again, because I recognized the truth of finding self and working on self, I was aware that I began to attract people who felt and thought like me. Like attracts like. Always be mindful of this.

Because I could sense others' energy and be more aware of my surroundings, the universe guided me to bless others with books they could read for self-help and expand the mind. As mentioned before, the Heart Chakra, when open, can cause you to not only love yourself but also others as well as being more kind. All of the Chakras were at work. I was guided by my intuition, "Third eye." I was kind, "Heart." I was speaking my truth, "Throat," by calling their names to give the gift. I felt the pleasure, "Sacral," in giving. I could feel the connection, "Crown," of the universe while giving. I felt I was standing my ground,

"Root," in passing the gift of knowledge I believe in. I also felt confident, "Solar plexus," that the book I was giving would help these loving people. See, as stated before, all these Chakras intertwine with each other, working together.

Since I had finally manifested my dream job, I began wanting to be a manager. I found myself daydreaming of sitting in a manager's seat. The calls were sometimes tough, so that really had my energy moving, creating a strong emotion for the desire to be in charge. This then opened doors for me too, instead, monitor calls. I was so excited about no longer having to take calls and deal with agitated customers. I felt even more excited about going to work. I was always on time and there, ready to work. Some months down the road, the client stated they needed assistant managers for our location. This opened doors for me to become an assistant manager and also gave me the opportunity for a pay increase.

I was filled with enthusiasm at this point. I found myself in another training except for this time; it was for management. The position had me back on the phone but only for escalated calls. I still had more freedom and time away from calls if front-line representatives would de-escalate the call, which is sometimes hard to do and led me to practice who I received on a call as these calls were inbound. I will talk more about that later in this chapter.

After training, I handled being an assistant manager well. I must admit, it did come with some big responsibilities. For instance, making sure I provided correct information to representatives before they assisted the customer. That is pretty much in every corporate business anyone could encounter. After a while, I noticed that another co-worker appeared to show some dislike toward me. I was already a little used to it, as I experienced a lot of different personalities once being promoted to monitoring phone calls, but this was different. I did not expect this specific co-worker to express dislike and attitude toward me. It started to make me feel uncomfortable, but I knew what I needed to do to correct it.

How I calmed a moody co-worker. To start, I found myself going home after work feeling bothered and overwhelmed by the low, negative energy I was absorbing from this co-worker. As assistant managers, we all sat in the same row. So, I was sitting in this energy for eight to nine hours a day and sometimes more with possible overtime. I am an empath. Empath beings are extremely sensitive individuals who can sense another's emotions or vibrations. Some can literally hear others' thoughts. Yes, this has to do with Chakras when they are completely open and charged, so this varies depending on the individual.

I have been able to sense others' true emotions since I was a child. That ability can come and go like day and night. It can sometimes depend on the situation and person. Remember, Chakras can be open, and they can be closed for many different reasons. It all starts with a thought. Once I was home, my sons were off to bed, and my husband off to work, I would take a hot shower while imagining the day's negativity going down the drain along with the soap suds and water. I would then get out of the shower, thanking the universe for always providing and for protecting me from negativity. I would then put my comfortable sleep clothes on, light a white candle, and take out my stone to charge from the candle's light. I would sit in a comfortable position after recharging my safe stone.

While holding my stone in the palm of my hand, I would first focus on my energy by thanking the universe again, inhaling and counting to three, then exhaling and counting to three, four, or six. I would do this until I was fully relaxed. I then stated affirmations such as I Am safe. I Am protected. I Am one with pure positive source energy. I Am Confident. I attract pure positive energy. I Am Love. I Am loved. I Am that I Am. Namaste'. I again inhaled, counting to three, four, or six, and visualized white light pouring onto all my Chakras like a waterfall. I would then inhale counting to three and exhale counting to three, four, or six and end with a sample thank you. Namaste'.

Then, while still holding and now looking and twirling my stone, I asked the universe to send my co-worker light. I would ask that whatever it was that was bothering the co-worker, for it to be resolved, fixed. I would then say, "All is well," and go off to sleep.

This was not done every night. I would do this practice only when feeling extremely low. I then went about my day, thanking the universe for protection and for helping my co-worker. I was not counting days on how long this took to manifest; it just happened. One day I went to work, and that co-worker's attitude was completely changed toward me and others. I was relieved. That co-worker smiled more often and even complimented my outfit or hair more often. See. This can be done in any situation and not only for co-workers. This, again, is my experience. Other co-workers may not have known or noticed this co-worker's attitude toward me, but I did.

There is a lot I notice in my day, and I understand the power and importance of shifting my attention and, therefore, attraction. Approximately a month later, I again started to feel negativity, but this time from two managers. I started to sense that I was being targeted for possibly being demoted. Before going to HR, I instead went to another manager to explain what I was sensing as I could see I was always closely watched as though I was doing something wrong. As stated before, I was always at work and on time when scheduled. I was a true team player. I saw myself climbing heights with this company. But clearly, the universe had something else in mind. After going to this other manager to explain what I was experiencing, he noticed it, too, along with other managers and my assistant co-workers. So, we all went to HR, one by one, to explain the situation.

While this case was open, I felt more support from others regarding the issue I was facing. When going home, I again would meditate and ask as well as give gratitude to the universe for protection. I did not want to lose my position over what I considered nonsense, but I knew then and know now that everything happens for a reason. After the case was finished, I was demoted. They agreed that the demotion was accurate because I provided misinformation to a representative, but they did not agree with targeting employees based on witnesses being managers as well as my co-workers.

After this experience, I was highly disappointed with the company. I felt it was not fair to just demote me. I felt I should have only been written up with a warning. I was then back on calls with frontline representatives. I found myself crying and no longer happy with this dream job. I started to feel guidance that it was time to let go and move on. Although I was demoted, one of the managers no longer worked at the company, and the other moved on to another client in the building. Before they went their separate ways, I still spoke to them and wished them well, showing all was forgiven.

There were rumors that the client wanted to expand at our location, so I was asked if I wanted my position back. At first, I did, but at this point was acing my regular inbound calls and did not care whether I remained as a frontline representative or not. I was going with the flow. I accepted the fact that I was demoted. I was at peace but still knew that the time was coming to move on. So, I again took action to attempt to get a new job at another company. The interview went well from my perspective, but I did not get the job.

I was disappointed at first but thought to myself, "Do I actually want to leave one stressful corporate company for another?" Even though I handled my calls like a pro, I was also becoming stressed. I was getting tired of dealing with angry and agitated customers. So, I once again went home to do what I do best, work on self and meditate to refocus my attention on positivity.

I would go home after a long day of work. As mentioned before, I would take a hot shower while visualizing the worries from the day going down the drain with the soap suds and water. After putting on comfortable clothes and lighting a white candle, I would then meditate and give thanks to the universe for helping me to attract loving and kind customers. I again did not do this every day as every day was not always tough. I would do this after encountering an angry customer or when I noticed that I was attracting complicated customers.

Once arriving to work, I would state, "Everything is always working out for me. Today, I will have a good day." When doing this, I noticed how I was attracting more reasonable customers. Once I mastered this, change came knocking on the door. A new client was taking over our location, so I was in training once again. This time we focused on business customers. Since these customers were business, some things needed to be done right away. Others wanted it done right, so they did not mind the time it may take to get their requests done. Of course, there were still some complicated customers, but I must honestly say, most were patient, polite, and professional.

I then found myself attracting customers that knew of this universal law as well. While I was processing orders, I had a customer ask, "Porsha, have you ever heard of the Law of Attraction? or "Porsha, are you aware of the power of thought?" This would make my call flow so smoothly. We would talk while still being professional, like good friends. Then my call would end with, "It's been a pleasure talking to you, Porsha." One day I had a customer call, and while I was processing her request, she stated that she was grateful that I could assist and that I was going far—even outside of the client I was taking calls for. I knew once again this was someone who was connected and in tune with her Sixth sense and Crown Chakras. While she talked, I could feel the universe, my archangels, and guides at play there. I felt that butterfly feeling in my Solar plexus Chakra, and it was as if the hairs on my body stood up because, again, I knew the time had come to move on.

Since working for the new client, my schedule had changed from regular eight-hour shifts to ten-hour shifts, but I had more days off. Because of my long hours at work, I had cut back on meditating and found myself extremely tired. I no longer felt like my high, authentic self. I later found out that my husband and I were pregnant again. We both were surprised and excited. Because I have two boys, we were hoping to have a girl. This time, compared to my pregnancy with my younger son Mikah, I was working instead of being home with my feet up. It was not until I became pregnant that I started to miss days from work. At this point, I was so over having to work for this company, maybe more so than previously. I was always hungry, sick, and tired. There were many occasions when I would get in my car, preparing to drive off, and my husband would catch me drenched in tears, and he would tell me to call in.

Despite the way I felt, I did not quit because I was dedicated. As stated before, I had become extremely stressed, especially while being pregnant. Everyone was so excited about my new pregnancy. Co-workers, managers, and family were all excited, and everyone was rooting for a girl. I even noticed the closeness my younger son had toward me. Both of my sons were highly aware that I was carrying another child. One day while at home, my husband and I asked Kyle and Mikah what they were hoping to have, a little brother or sister? Mikah, my youngest, stated with confidence, "She's a girl!"

I remember saying to him, "I hope so, big boy," with a smile on my face, knowing that I have seen this before. Since he stated that our unborn was a girl, we all decided to call our unborn baby a girl. In a way, I still was playing it safe by stating, "I'm fine either way, as long as he or she is safe and healthy." However, due to having three boys back-to-back in the past, I still was unsure that my youngest was right.

My husband and I thought of some names, but I had one in mind. I kept it to myself as four other women, my sister included, were pregnant as well. That made this pregnancy even more special. This was my sister's first child and my first nephew on my mother's side. After a few months of hoping for a girl, it was finally time to find out the gender of my unborn child. My husband and I went to the appointment to discover that we were having a girl, just as my youngest stated. We all were excited. I could not wait to share the news. My family was excited, and my coworkers were excited. Finally, my girl!

After losing my first daughter from my previous relationship and because I could no longer bear the stress of work, I decided to go part-time. I knew I was feeling the way I did toward work because it was time for me to let it go. It was only in a matter of time. After I put in my request, I remember waiting for quite some time before finally being approved. I will never forget. It was a Friday, and I was just told by my manager, who had been working so diligently to get my part-time schedule approved, that the company had finally approved my request. I remember being so relieved that I would no longer have to sit for hours, hungry and talking to complicated customers based on my own emotions of no longer wanting to work there. With that being said, I remember leaving work that Friday feeling so burnt out from the day of constant talking and hiding my emotions to keep customers satisfied.

The following Sunday, on October 27, I woke up feeling fine. I had eaten breakfast and decided to watch TV with my husband. I suddenly was in pain and felt I needed to use the bathroom. I began to bleed and was beginning to worry. My husband called the ambulance to tell them what was happening. They came to rush me to the hospital for further assistance. After all the confusion about what was going on with my bleeding and pain, I was sent for an emergency C-section.

After finally waking up from the procedure, I awakened to the sad news of losing my baby girl. Because of the love, I had developed for Gaia, Nature, I named her Naiytur. I was so heartbroken. I called my work to give them the sad news and took time off to allow myself to heal physically, mentally, and spiritually. During my time off, I felt so relieved to not have to get up early to go and do what I no longer was excited to do. I spent more time with my sons and grieved with my husband.

A couple of weeks after my loss, I had a follow-up exam. While my husband and I sat in the waiting room, I happen to notice a red cardinal fluttering outside of the window. It began to tap on the window with its beak. I told my husband to look. We both were so amazed as we knew that was our Naiytur saying, "All is well." She came as my favorite bird to remind Mommy and Daddy that she is still here. This made me cry in both amazement and sadness, but I knew my baby was well.

Months later, after the new year of "2020," it was time for me to return to work. It was so hard returning without my baby girl moving around in my belly. I was still grieving and found myself running to the bathroom crying at the thought of her being gone. I still felt the urge to let go of my dream job but continued to hold on. When returning to work, the atmosphere was different as a lot of co-workers no longer worked for the company, and calls were extremely slow. By the time February came, Corona was spreading all over the world. So eventually, in March, I finally had the opportunity to work from home. I was beginning to feel excited about work again. I was finally doing what I envisioned. I manifested my dream job. Although I was later demoted, I manifested the managing position, and now I was working from home.

I again found out that I was pregnant. My husband and I were happy, but we still grieved for Naiytur. Things were a little better this pregnancy because I did not have to wake up to beat the morning traffic to go to a building. I was able to literally wake up, brush my teeth, and go downstairs to receive calls for work. On most days, I did not even bother to do my hair. I was excited to experience how it felt to be able to just get up and go. After a month or two, and after some changes were done with management at my company, I found myself feeling stressed. I no longer found pleasure in waking up to take calls for work from home. I was also receiving complicated calls, and days were once again busy. Although I still had my part-time shift, I again felt it was time to let my manifested dream job go. I kept fighting this feeling, and even knowing it was the universe stating it is time, I kept holding on.

One day I went to my doctor's office for a regular checkup. This day was special because we were finding out what we were having. Because of the rapid Corona spread, I had to go to appointments alone. On this day, instead of finding out the gender, we instead received news that we had lost another baby. My husband and I were very devastated once again. If we were having another girl, we were going to name her Sage. At this point, between losing Naiytur and Sage, I was feeling numb, but this time in a low-vibrational way. I once again took time off from work for six weeks to continue to grieve and to work on myself mentally and spiritually.

This time, I did things that brought me joy, such as watching comedy and doing things with my sons. I did not meditate much, but I did continue to state affirmations throughout my day, such as I Am healed. I Am well. I Am Love. I Am loved. I Am happy. As the days went by, I found myself counting down days to when it was time to go back to work, and as I did that, I started to feel sad because I knew work was not as pleasing anymore as it once was. Before I knew it, it was time to clock back in for work.

To help me to enhance my thoughts and feelings about work, and since I was working from home, I took it upon myself to turn on some loving music, light a white candle, and open some windows. I would also put clothes on and do my hair. While getting dressed, I would give thanks to the universe for blessing me with the opportunity to work from home. I would state again, "Today will be a good day. I will attract loving, peaceful customers. All is well." When doing this, my day went so smoothly. My desk was by the same back window where I had the hawk visitation from the previous chapter. I had a view of the red cardinals and blue jays landing in the trees and grass in my backyard. As stated before, I love Nature, and now when seeing red cardinals with my daughter in mind, I saw a message stating, "All is well." So, even if I was not having a good day at times, I was always reminded that "All is well."

In September, my city experienced hurricane Sally. I remember being up that night listening and feeling the winds of Gaia beat the walls of my home and hearing her sing through the windows. I silently gave thanks to the universe for keeping me, my family, and my home safe. After the storm passed, I noticed how I felt different mentally and spiritually. I began to read more again and found myself being fed with new information from my guides. I, more than ever before, found myself ready to let go of what no longer served me for my highest good. I have always believed that storms symbolize change, and that is exactly how I felt. Changed.

The client for the company I worked for was ready for a change too and decided to end our work for business customers but needed assistance with regular consumer customers. The company stated that a full-time schedule was mandatory to keep employment. I was working part-time and could not, and would not, work the new schedule that was given. Outside of work, because of the coronavirus, my youngest was schooling remotely and needed my full attention. My husband was working more than twelve hours a day. So, the choice was made, and the time had come to finally let go. Three years later, on the same day that I was hired, October 2, my manifested dream job ended. I am full of love and gratitude for the wonderful opportunity this company has given me. So many ups and downs I have had with them, and I have no regrets. If there is a dream you have, go for it! Give your intention and attention to it, and it shall manifest.

Chapter sixteen

MY PERSONAL STONES OF POWER

Before manifesting my dream job, I was guided and introduced to stones and crystals. While working with Archangel Raphael, I grew a love for Nature because I felt the connection to Gaia, earth. I found myself being drawn to a specific stone, seeing tigers, and hearing "The Eye of the Tiger" song every time I turned the radio on. I would then hear it on television during a movie or commercial. I cannot recall seeing or hearing someone mention it on a streaming radio show I would listen to, but I remember seeing it for the first time and felt a constant urge to purchase one for myself. It is called "Tiger's eye." It is a stone that can bring balance, good luck, money, success, confidence, and protection. It is said that this stone also has physical healing abilities for the throat. It can help with anxiety and fear. This is one of my personal favorites and is the stone I used in the previous chapter when emotionally healing myself while encountering a moody co-worker, as well as when interviewing for my dream job.

Like charging phone batteries, you must charge your stones. There are several ways to charge this stone. You can charge it from the sun's light, as this is the stone I was admiring while on the beach in the previous chapter. You can also charge it by candlelight, or you could charge it using smoke by burning sage or frankincense incense. You would want to keep this afloat, as when it is used, you must recharge. I recharge when I feel it is time. You will know. Give attention to the way you feel when holding it and be aware of your thoughts.

The next stone I found myself attracted to while monitoring calls at my dream job is called "Sodalite." This stone can provide truth. It is also known to treat conditions that may affect the throat and voice. It can help you accept the truth of something after becoming aware of it. It can also help you to accept who you truly are by no longer judging yourself. It can help you to feel more connected to the universe. I choose to cleanse and recharge this stone by moonlight or smoke, again using sage or frankincense incense.

The next stone, more considered a crystal, is the "Clear quartz crystal." I was guided to this crystal after losing both my babies Naiytur and Sage. It is said that this crystal can heal and unblock all Chakras. This crystal is known for healing emotionally and physically. I like to charge this crystal in the sun or moonlight. I sometimes like to place it in the window and notice how more peaceful my home feels. I also prefer lighting white candles while charging or using this crystal.

Lastly, my next favorite is "Amber." One morning, I awoke to hearing constantly, "Amber." I kept hearing it so loud and once found myself awakening while saying "amber." I had also noticed that my youngest, Mikah, would call out that name while playing or watching one of his favorite TV shows. I asked him who was Amber. He responded by saying it was a children's show he had been watching. It had come to my knowledge that this is a stone that has the ability, like the tiger's eye, to help you attract money, good luck, confidence, and can help you balance emotions. It is also known to protect. It is said that its physical abilities can heal diseases from the body. This stone can also enhance happiness. I choose to charge this stone in the sun.

You can use any stone of your choosing, including those that I have not named. Always go by the way you think and feel when it comes to choosing your stones or crystals. It will call out to you as you call out to it. You will attract it. Please know, sometimes you will be guided to bless someone with a stone of their own, but it is up to them on how they will go about using it. Namaste'.

Chapter seventeen

MY BELIEF THAT NO ONE EVER TRULY DIES

Because of my experiences with loved ones who have crossed over and my witness to a gifted, intelligent child, my brother, I believe that no one truly dies. In this chapter, I will explain the experiences I have had with loved ones who have crossed over to the non-physical realm. Some of these experiences I have already mentioned in previous chapters. I feel in my soul and during meditation that we all originally came from space—somewhere out in the universe non-physically. I believe that is our original existence. Some of us have chosen to come in many other lifetimes in the past.

I believe we choose to come physically before being physically born. I believe we choose the families we want or need to be born into, and because of the Law of Attraction, it is so. I believe we already know what it is we have come to do and accomplish before incarnation, but we forget, at least most of us. If we allow it and welcome it, we will find our way back to our original state of being. Our original state of being is knowing our own strength, knowing the power starts with self, and knowing what we came to be, do, create, and how to fulfill our destiny as we move through life physically. In doing this, we heal ourselves from the pain we go through or find ourselves in. In doing this, we help heal others. In doing this, we help heal Gaia, Mother Earth. In doing this, we please the universe, our souls, our ancestors, and therefore ourselves.

With that being said, I have been asked on many occasions, "Porsha, how did you get your name? Was a Porsche your mother's favorite car?" I would laugh and say no. A Porsche is my favorite car, but here's why my mother named me Porsha. While my mother was pregnant with me, she was told she was having a boy. She had a baby shower and was given clothes and such for the boy she thought she was having. Then the day had finally come. Shortly after her high school graduation, she went into labor. As it was a long process, she fell asleep. She first had a dream that a snake had crawled up her private area. This dream frightened her. She awakened, then fell back to sleep and dreamt of a huge Jesus who wore purple and gold, like the robes the prophet once wore at the church I once attended. She stated that Jesus was holding a baby, but she was a girl. She awakened and thought about that dream hoping it was not so, and was confused, not understanding what that dream meant.

She then fell back to sleep and dreamt that my father was there with her in the hospital. In the dream, like before, instead of having a boy, she had a girl. She said while she and my father were admiring their new baby girl, my father stated, "We should name her Porsha." She was then awakened to push as she had fully dilated. My mother went through the entire process of giving birth to her first child, then just as she had dreamt, out came a baby girl. I can imagine the surprised look on her face when being told, "It's a girl!" She then named me "Porsha." I cannot recall my age when she told me how I got my name, but I was so tired of people asking, and not knowing at the time as a little girl, I often wondered why Porsha? There was a time when I did not know there was such a car—not until I was nine or ten. So, because of my mother's experience and why she named me "Porsha," and along with my other experiences that I am going to tell you in this chapter, I, therefore, believe that no one ever truly dies and existed before being physically alive.

I believe that it was me who came to my mother in the form of my father to tell her that my name is Porsha. Let me go back to my friend who saw his crossing over before it happened. As stated before, after his passing, I had felt guilty and sad about letting him go for an old fling. One day, before I lost my first child Aaliyah and before I found out I was even pregnant, I dreamed I was in a hilly, grassy field. It was so sunny out and breezy. It felt so real that I could feel the breeze on my face. Sitting in front of me was my friend, and behind him stood the person whom he was with the day he passed over. I knew that this was who it was but could not make out the person's face, but I could sense a smile as that person stood from afar to give us space. I started to pour my heart out. I told him that I was sorry for letting him go and that I was sorry for what happened to him. I told him how I felt guilty and that I felt it was my fault for letting him go. I told him that I missed him so much. He suddenly smiled. I instantly felt the guilt go away. I then said with relief, "I have wanted to tell you this for the longest time."

I awakened from my dream, which was actually a visitation. From that point on, I no longer felt guilty. His smile told me that he is okay and wants me to be okay too. I still missed him dearly after that visit. He was on my mind all day. As mentioned before, I also had a visitation from him before losing my first baby girl Aaliyah. I have come to know that my friend will forever be with me if both parties allow. I strongly feel it was also him that brought my husband and me together. The church I once attended had all his close family members, including his mom, which he at one point when here physically wanted to introduce me to her but never got a chance, but he did while in the non-physical realm. That, too, was confirmation that he was at peace and wanted me to be as well. I dreamt of him recently and realized that it was his passing-over anniversary. What that did was give me the thought, the idea, to write this chapter. I love you, friend. You will forever live, my brother, in all things, in all hearts, and all life.

One day when I was approximately fourteen or fifteen, I was at home alone, and the doorbell rang. Immediately, I looked out the window, but no one was there. I assumed that I could not see them from my point of view. I then opened the front door. No one was there, but to find out later that day, it was my grandfather's birthday. My grandfather passed when I was only three. I have heard so many stories about the love he had for me. For so many years, I wished he were around physically to tell me everything he knew. My grandfather was a policeman, a farmer, a man of his word who loved the ladies but finally grew to hold one specifically in his heart, whom I call my bamma. Bamma was his most recent wife up until he crossed over. That made her my step-grandmother, but I prefer to call her my grandmother. While married to my bamma, my grandfather eventually gained custody of my mother when she was a child. I called her bamma because I could not pronounce grandma.

Speaking of my bamma. One year around Thanksgiving. I had dreamt that my aunt, who is my bamma's daughter, was baking a cake while my bamma watched as though she was telling her what ingredients to use. My husband and I did not originally know what we were going to do that year or to whose house we would choose to go for Thanksgiving. We ended up at that aunt's apartment who had made a homemade lemon cake for the first time. She stated that her mother, which again is my bamma, use to make a homemade lemon cake all the time, and she wanted to give it a try that year. Her mother had recently passed, so she kept her ashes close while making the cake. That dream was a vision showing me that my bamma was there, guiding her through each step of the recipe to help get it right. I was in awe when told how my aunt made the homemade lemon cake, which was good, by the way, in knowing I had that vision.

As mentioned before, one day after losing my second child Kylen, my mother called me, stating a cousin whom we have not heard nor seen in years told her that his mother, who had passed years prior, said to tell me to keep praying. Before she passed, I remember her being able to see things that had not yet manifested. I even remember her knowing that one of my cousins, who was her niece, was pregnant when she was attempting to keep it a secret. My aunt was a loving, caring person full of laughter and silliness, had class, and managed to graduate college before crossing over. She was a woman of God. I sense my aunt still has a lot to teach as she was also a Sunday school teacher. I sense my aunt now knows that there is so much more to life as her energy is still strong and around to teach just that. I love you, Aunty. Thanks for the encouragement.

And lastly, my loving daughter Naiytur. As mentioned before, while sitting in the waiting room for my follow-up, I happen to look out the window of my doctor's office. A red cardinal, my favorite bird, was fluttering outside of the window. It then started to tap at the window. I told my husband to look as the red cardinal continued to flutter outside of the window. We both managed to walk over to the window. The red cardinal continued to flutter outside the window as if it knew it had our attention. We were then called to the back for my follow-up. By the time we were done, the red cardinal was gone. It is said that when red cardinals arrive, it is a loved one who has passed over, telling you, "All is well." Red cardinals also symbolize good luck, romance, the number twelve (which is said in numerology to symbolizes completion), creativity, and expression. Red cardinals are also known to be spiritual messengers.

At Naiytur's burial, my husband's son, Trae, did the brief eulogy at his sister's burial. Right after he was done, I again was in tears as I felt I was saying goodbye. Immediately, he stated while pointing up, "Look!" My husband, family, friends, and I all looked up to see the bird formation that flew over our heads. I cried in sadness but also in the release of confirmation that Naiytur was okay and came to do what she promised to do: to inspire, bless, and bring her family closer. Naiytur, you are my light in the dark that I have always looked for. I now know and understand the bigger picture of physically losing you, then later Sage. You two brought the icing to the cake. I had lost myself, found myself, lost myself again to only find myself finding myself. Thank you for all the wonderful experiences you bring me. Mommy and Daddy love you, always.

I want to end this chapter with this. It has been confirmed to me that, as stated previously, my husband and I have done this before. We are what are known to be twin flames or kindred souls. This explains why we recognized each other when we first met. We then gave ourselves the challenge of having to ignore the opinions and minds of others by taking charge of our own situation and turn our wounds into wisdom. Sadly, things do not always go as we hope and only for the greater good of all. My husband and I are currently going through some hard times, but may the battle continue to teach and help us grow. I do not know who, when, or where we were in our past lifetimes together, but I do know this, we are one. We were meant to find each other once again to finish whatever we started in the past. Know that we are all souls first before we are human beings. We are non-physical before we are physical beings. We are dark as well as light. We are all things, so choose wisely. Choose what benefits you for your highest good. Everything in all things is life. Even while here non-physically, my loved ones are still able to communicate and be of assistance. So are yours. Love. Focus on love, and so be it.

Chapter eighteen

MEET THE ORISHAS

After all the experiences I mentioned in the previous chapters, during meditation, I sensed the universe stating, "Now you know who you are spiritually; it is time you know who you are physically." I found myself wanting to know who I am physically and where do my physical roots lie. One of who I consider being today's greats, Beyonce, came out with, *The Gift* album, which she later did a visual of that album called "Black is King," based on Disney's, *The Lion King*. As a child, *The Lion King* was always my favorite Disney movie. The storyline has always touched me so deeply that words cannot explain. I listened to *The Gift* for hours without skipping a tune.

I took note of how Bey seems to be different. I could sense a strong energy from her and became curious to know what or who she was channeling. I then became aware that she was channeling a powerful Orisha, also known as the goddess Oshun. This was once again something completely new to me. When I think of the Orishas, I think of them like the Archangels, God, angelic beings that are here in the universe non-physically by choice to assist those that are seeking their truth. It has been said that each Orisha has its own individual, human-like characteristics. In this book, because I believe in the Law of Attraction, I will focus more on their loving characteristics.

Who Am I? Why Am I here? were the two questions that began my journey of finding, *My Own Strength*. Since becoming aware of this feminine source of energy, Oshun (some prefer Osun), once again, I would notice the aura yellow, but this time it was while watching a movie or tv show. That color stood out as though it was stating, "Look at me." I found myself noticing and being more attracted to sunflowers. In my experience, this was Orisha's way of communicating to me based on what I was already experiencing with the Archangels. I became as attracted to her as she to me. Please keep in mind the power of the Law of Attraction. Because I gave my attention to what I have learned is called an Orisha, a new journey began. Like attracts like.

I did some research before welcoming her like I had done with everything else because this was completely new to me. Again, please note that it is always important to work on self first by prayer and meditation, asking and thanking the universe for protection before allowing any energy, thing, and/or person into your energy field. We are like magnets. We attract who and what we are. When we are happy, we attract happiness. When we are brave, we attract courage. When we are confident, we attract confidence. When we love ourselves, we attract people who love us, and so on. Therefore, I have experienced all this, which I speak of in this book. I am constantly working on Me. Self. Sometimes we may find ourselves in situations that are not necessarily to our liking, but we know this is a part of life, but we do not have to remain there.

While cleansing my home with incense first, then a white candle or candles, I found myself welcoming Oshun into my energy field. I then welcomed her again during meditation and asked if she could teach me more about who she is and why we have crossed paths. Since welcoming, I have learned that Nigeria runs deep through my veins. I have learned that I come from warriors and kings. I have also learned that I am physically many other things, but my focus in this final chapter is about the African Yoruba belief in Orishas. I have also attracted books and information from my research.

Oshun loves sunflowers and is an Orisha of love. Oshun helps enhance love in relationships and marriages. Oshun also can enhance your love for yourself, and with the Law of Attraction, it can help attract more love to your life. Like my Archangel Jophiel, Oshun is also a goddess of beauty. I love to thank Oshun and Jophiel for helping me to continue to beautify my life and soul. Once again, since being in contact with this Orisha, I have found myself taking my beauty to another level. I have grown to love turbans, or in other words, headwraps. In Africa, they are known as gele. I have never been a huge fan of makeup, but found myself wearing eyeliner "Egyptian style" and crystal or amber color lip gloss. Since welcoming Oshun into my life, I have also found myself able to express myself more lovingly.

Oshun can also help attract success, money, and abundance. Oshun also likes amber, and her day is Saturday. Yellow symbolizes this Orisha as her energy is very vibrant. Honey and bees are good symbols of this Orisha. So, throughout my day, while I am out in Nature and I see bees or yellow and sunflowers, I give thanks to Oshun and the universe. I then state affirmations such as I Am Love. I Am loved. I Am healthy. I Am wealthy. I Am money. I Am that I Am. Oshun also helps to promote happiness, so I also include the affirmation, I Am happy. It has been said that this Orisha is also good to call on when working on the Heart and the Solar plexus Chakra. Because of that, I also include the affirmation, I Am confident. While meditating, I prefer to light a yellow

"Crown of Success" candle in honor of this beautiful and wonderful Orisha.

After Oshun made herself known, during meditation, I found myself thinking about the ocean and missed it as we were still in the middle of a pandemic. I chose to stay home and away from crowded locations. I love music in all shapes and forms. I later thought about how there were no good female rappers that I could relate to. One day after reading, I decided to turn on the TV to watch some music videos. There was a music video by a rapper I had never heard of. I loved her style and became inspired to search for more of her music. This rapper mentioned a name that sounded so familiar, but I did not know much about it and decided again to research. Yemaya. This Orisha is also known as a river goddess in Nigeria. It is said that when her people were stored on the slave ships, Mother Yemaya went with them and became the goddess of the ocean, widely known as the mother of the ocean. Yemaya is also known as Yemoja. The moon and stars are symbols of Mother Yemaya. Her color is white and is also known to be blue. She loves pearls and everything that comes from the ocean. She also loves flowers and fragrances.

As you can see, by turning on my TV at the right moment, with the urge and desire to watch music videos, the Law of Attraction was at work, guiding me to this music artist. It intended to lead me to this specific Orisha because I wanted to know who I Am, spiritually and physically. Yemaya also helps with nurturing children and others. It has been said that she protects pregnant women and helps women by making sure they are safe when giving birth. Now I understand why I have always been drawn to the ocean, Mother Yamaya. During meditation, I thank Mother Yemaya for nurturing me, especially during hard times. I also thank her for helping me to be a better nurturer to my children and husband.

It only makes sense that these two specific Orishas made themselves known, as I am a Cancer, the Zodiac sign of nurturing, caring, and love. Water is the element. I later found out that these two Orisha's, Oshun and Yemaya like to work together. They both are Orishas of water. Oshun being the river, and Yemaya being the ocean. It is said Yemaya gave Oshun the rivers so that she would have her own kingdom. After Yemaya made herself known, like before with my archangels, other Orishas made themselves known one by one.

Very shortly after being released from my manifested dream job, on October 16, I decided to go to one of my favorite stores for a pickup. When picking up items, there is a code that must be given to the employee for identification. The number was 7337. I then went home and decided to take the trash out. My dumpster was in the street as it was trash day for my neighborhood. I dumped my trash, then took it around the garage area of my home. When walking towards the front of my garage, there was a loud noise that sounded like an airplane flying low over my head. This day was windy as it was autumn and normally windy during this time of the year. Because of the loud sound, I looked up. It was not an airplane but sixteen hawks flying, swarming, or hovering over my home. I counted all sixteen twice to make sure I had it right. It was as though they knew they had my attention because they had spread out for me to make sure I counted correctly. There was no airplane; that was the wind blowing hard in my ears, blowing my African earrings, and guiding me to look up.

Earlier that day, a bluejay was sitting on the fence in my backyard, which immediately reminded me of the hawk visitation mentioned in chapter fourteen. It has come to my knowledge that this was Ogun. Like Archangel Michael, I call him the Orisha of protection. It has been said that Ogun comes to teach hard lessons as a tough father would. He is a protector and a warrior. Ogun is known to be a god of metal and iron. He symbolizes truth, patience, justice, and war. He influences technology. His color is green but can vary as some believe it to be red or black. Animals that symbolize him are hawks and tigers. His numbers are three and seven. It has been said the Root Chakra can be focused on when meditating and giving thanks to the universe and this Orisha, Ogun. I give thanks to Archangel Michael and Ogun for protecting me and my family and household. I thank these beings during meditation and throughout my day.

After becoming aware of Ogun, I noticed I would see 321 a lot. While going about my day, I happen to look at the clock, and it would be 3:21. I even placed an order for some handmade oil to help enhance my attraction. I happen to look at the expiration date; it stated 3/21. I also would often see 3, 33, and 333. It has come to my knowledge that this was Elegua. Elegua is the Orisha of messages. He is also known as "The messenger." In the Yoruba language, he is known as Elegbara. Since I have a love for burning incense, candles, and sage; I needed a new lighter. I asked my husband while he was out at work if he could bring one home. My husband came home with two that were so unique. One of them had a woman holding Gaia, Earth in her hands. The other had a key with a heart above printed on the front. I was amazed because Elegua is also known as the key-keeper. He holds the keys to communicate with Orishas and life in the non-physical realm. His number is three.

Elegua also helps to open doors for success and can assist with making decisions that best serve you for your highest good. His colors are known to be red and black. When cleansing my home, I tend to thank both Elegua and Ogun for protection and for allowing positivity to flow through and around my home. I welcome peace, love, laughter, and happiness into my home. I prefer burning incense by the front entryway of my home in honor of this Orisha, giving thanks unto the universe and him. When seeing blue jays, I think of this Orisha. It is also said that Ogun and Elegua often work together.

The next Orisha that I have come to love and know is Oya. Oya is an Orisha of change. Wind, tornadoes, hurricanes, and storms are symbols of this Orisha. As I mentioned previously, after hurricane Sally I felt vastly different in my energy and was ready to let what no longer served me go. Oya's number is nine. It is said her color is brown or burgundy. This Orisha brought change into my life. Like the rest of my guides, this Orisha helped me to manifest this book into reality when before, I did not believe in myself to write a book, especially about my life, as I can be a very private person in general. But it's come to my knowledge that my story needed to be shared, as I believe it not only helps me but others too.

I was once told that I needed to let go of things and people so that I could receive my blessings. This is what Oya is about. Letting go of what is old to receive the new. One day, I decided to take my sister some food and dropped it off at my mother's. On my way, while at a stoplight, a van pulled beside me with exactly that printed on the side "Let go of what is old to receive the new." I knew immediately to give thanks to the universe and Oya for change and newness. When thanking the universe and the Orishas during meditation, I thank Oya for change and protection as she is also a warrior for women and justice.

This next Orisha is the reason I was born with the gift of singing and dancing. Sango, also known as Shango or Chango, works together with Oya during storms as he is known to be the god of thunder and music. When first being made aware of this Orisha, I did not understand why we were attracting each other as when researching him, his characteristics at first did not suit me, or so I thought. This Orisha made himself known by me by constantly hearing and seeing his name while I was meditating and studying the others. I did not understand until during a night of meditation after I put my sons to bed. "What is it that you want?" I asked. "Why am I sensing your energy? I feel I have nothing to do with you, but I must because you are here." I then heard music. I said, "Oooooh. I should have known—my first love."

Sango is known to beat drums, dance, and musically communicate with others. It is said that thunder is a good symbol for him. When you think of Sango, think of Thor, as Sango is also a warrior. Sango with Oya helps to create and bring change into one's life. Sango helps to bring musical ideas to shore. My husband one day ordered a music book. I immediately was excited after days of meditating and finally welcoming Sango into my energy field. I knew this was Sango's way of saying, I am here and available.

My last Orisha was Obatala. Obatala is an Orisha of peace, knowledge, thoughts, and dreams. His number is eight. He is known to be the father of Orishas and human bodies. It is said he plays a part in "The breath of life." Obatala is the intellect and can help bring ideas and knowledge to shore. His color is white, and his day is Sunday. When honoring this Orisha, I wear white and give thanks for the intelligence which I seek and find. On Sundays, which I like to call "Day one," before becoming aware of Obatala, I found myself being guided to share personal knowledge and music from an artist that I have written about in this book to close loved ones. I later became aware that this was Obatala. Obatala, like my many other guides, helps me to focus and not only help and educate myself of this truth but also others who are willing and want to know and experience life on a new level of existence. Please keep in mind that to some, this Yoruba belief is a myth, but to me, due to my personal experience, the Yoruba beliefs are true. Truth is found in all religions everywhere and in all things, including ourselves. It is like puzzle pieces waiting to be found.

In Conclusion

Even though I have come to know and realize all these things I have written about, I still have so much to learn. There are still times of doubt and sometimes sadness. Just as night turns to day and day turns to night, I have learned that not only are we the light, happiness, and positivity, but we are also the darkness, sadness, and negativity. The universe has taught me to simply choose and allow. All in all, all is well.

Please be mindful of what you do daily—how you treat yourself and others and the decisions you make in your everyday life. Please know that it will all come back to you. You are attracting it. This is true whether you are aware of it or not. Because I am open to learning, I leave room to continue to grow. Never think you are too old, educated, or uneducated to learn something new. Be forever young. You are forever young. We are forever young.

After becoming aware of this information, practicing, and experiencing it, I found myself being more kind to myself and others. As mentioned before, when guided, I gave away books that helped me on this journey. So now I have presented my very own to you. I hope you enjoyed the pain, love, and warmth of my journey to find, *My Own Strength*. May this knowledge help you with yours. Please know, you do not have to wait to get to heaven to see God. Look in the mirror and all around you. God is here. This is *My Own Strength*. Namaste'. Ase'.

Glossary

THIS GLOSSARY IS IN THE ORDER OF MY STORY

Energy field - In physics; An electric field surrounds an electric charge; When another charged particle is placed in that region, it experiences an electric force that either attracts or repels it, which can reflect an aura.

Aura - A light that surrounds your physical body.

Vibration - A person's emotional state, the atmosphere of a place, or the associations of an object, as communicated to and felt by others.

Gaia - From ancient Greek, the personification of the earth. Named after a Greek goddess spelled Gaea.

Archangels - An angel of high rank.

Chakra - Wheel and refers to energy points in your body. Each of the centers of spiritual power in the human body.

Orisha - Any of several Gods in southern Nigeria. A manifestation of God. Like the Archangels, some believe that these spirits will give them help in life to assist with achieving the destiny that God planned for them before they were born.

Yoruba - A member of any of the Yoruba African people of the region. The language of the Yoruba and an official language of Nigeria.

Gele - A traditional Nigerian headwrap. It symbolizes empowerment and importance and is often worn for special occasions.

Give Gratitude

I want to thank the universe with all my spiritual guides, for guiding, and encouraging me to write my story for many to read and be inspired. Thank you, to my editors and book designer for helping me to bring this vision to life. And lastly, thank you James, for being one of the biggest lessons I could ever have. I love you. Namaste'. Ase'.

Please leave a review

I would love it if you could leave your honest review. Please feel free to leave a review on Amazon regarding your experience while reading *My Own Strength*.

www.ingramcontent.com/pod-product-compliance
Lightning Source LLC
Chambersburg PA
CBHW051702160426
43209CB00004B/989